Miss Thistlebottom's Hobgoblins

BOOKS BY

THEODORE M. BERNSTEIN

HEADLINES AND DEADLINES 1933, 1961
(*with Robert E. Garst*)

WATCH YOUR LANGUAGE 1958

MORE LANGUAGE THAT NEEDS WATCHING 1962

THE CAREFUL WRITER 1965

MISS THISTLEBOTTOM'S HOBGOBLINS 1971

MISS THISTLEBOTTOM'S HOBGOBLINS

*The Careful Writer's Guide
to the Taboos, Bugbears
and Outmoded Rules
of English Usage*

THEODORE M. BERNSTEIN

Farrar, Straus and Giroux

NEW YORK

FIRST NOONDAY PRINTING, 1973

Library of Congress catalog card number: 78–143299

Printed in the United States of America
Published simultaneously in Canada by
Doubleday Canada Ltd., Toronto
Designed by Herb Johnson

Repreve he dredeth never a del

Who that beset his wordis wel.

CHAUCER, "The Romaunt of the Rose"

Contents

A Word to the Whys

WHEN an author selects so unpronounceable and so unrememberable a title as *Miss Thistlebottom's Hobgoblins*, he owes a tiny part of the world an explanation. That debt will be met here and at once.

There are two reasons for the title. The first is the belief that a title so hard to pronounce and so hard to remember will be difficult to forget. The second reason is, naturally, a more serious one. The title is intended to suggest what the book is all about. It would have been a simple matter to settle on some such title as "A Dictionary of Contemporary Linguistic Dicta Lacking in Validity." That would have been completely explanatory, but would it have been better? Once you know that Miss Thistlebottom was your eighth-grade English teacher and that hobgoblins are bogies you have the whole story.

The purpose of this book is to lay to rest the superstitions that have been passed on from one generation to the next by teachers, by editors and by writers—prohibitions deriving from mere personal prejudice or from misguided pedantry or from a cold conservatism that would freeze the language if it could.

It is not difficult to substantiate such an indictment. When a newspaper editor outlaws such a phrase as "flying glass" on the ground that only birds and airplanes fly, that is personal prejudice. When grammarians of a bygone day arbitrarily decided that the split infinitive was vulgar, they were acting out of misguided pedantry. So scholarly an observer as George O. Curme tells us that "The insertion

of the adverb . . . between 'to' and the infinitive cannot
even in the strictest scientific sense be considered ungram-
matical," and at another point he says that "the split infinitive is an improvement of English expression." * When
a writer proclaims in print that it is wrong to say, "He appropriated his neighbor's horse to his own use," because
appropriate means to set apart, as a sum of money, for a
special purpose, he is attempting to freeze the word into
its ancient, original sense.

Does the attempt to lay such specters imply an attitude
of permissiveness? By no means. It is no more permissive to
strike down an editor's prohibition of the phrase "flying
glass" than it is to deny the right of the cop on the beat
to dictate what kind of shoes pedestrians should wear. There
is a perfectly legitimate code governing grammar, usage and
style, but the code is set up neither by cranks nor by know-
nothings. It derives from the generally accepted standards
of educated users of the language, often but not always influenced by what the masses say. What the code does not
need is ex cathedra injunctions by tinkerers who would
tamper with idioms, invent grammatical rules and clamp
word meanings into an everlasting vise. To resist them is
almost as necessary as to resist those who maintain that
whatever the people say is just fine. Both camps contribute
to confusion and imprecision. What we require is neither
a language that is cramped nor a language gone wild.

Books that are cited more than once in these pages are
designated by a short label. A list of them follows:

AMERICAN HERITAGE: *The American Heritage Dictionary
    of the English Language*, New York, American Herit-
    age Publishing Co., Inc., 1969.
AYRES: Alfred Ayres, *The Verbalist: A Manual De-*
* *Syntax*, p. 459.

voted to *Brief Discussions of the Right and the Wrong Use of Words and to Some Other Matters of Interest to Those Who Would Speak and Write with Propriety*, New York, D. Appleton & Co., 1882.

BIERCE: Ambrose Bierce, *Write It Right, A Little Blacklist of Literary Faults*, New York, Walter Neale, 1909.

BRYANT: Margaret M. Bryant, *Modern English and Its Heritage*, second edition, New York, The Macmillan Company, 1962.

BRYANT CAU: Margaret M. Bryant, *Current American Usage*, New York, Funk & Wagnalls Co., Inc., 1962.

COBBETT: *The English Grammar of William Cobbett Carefully Revised and Annotated by Alfred Ayres*, New York, D. Appleton and Company, 1891.

COWLES: *Cowles Volume Library*, New York, Cowles Book Company, Inc., 1969.

CURME: George O. Curme, *Syntax*, Boston, D. C. Heath and Company, 1931.

EVANS: Bergen Evans and Cornelia Evans, *A Dictionary of Contemporary American Usage*, New York, Random House, 1957.

EVANS CW: Bergen Evans, *Comfortable Words*, New York, Random House, 1962.

FOLLETT: Wilson Follett, *Modern American Usage, A Guide*, New York, Hill and Wang, 1966.

FOWLER: H. W. Fowler, *A Dictionary of Modern English Usage*, second edition, revised by Sir Ernest Gowers, London, Oxford University Press, 1965.

GREENOUGH: James Bradstreet Greenough and George Lyman Kittredge, *Words and Their Ways in English Speech*, Boston, Beacon Press, Beacon Paperback 1962. (First copyright 1900.)

HARPER'S: John B. Opdycke, *Harper's English Grammar*, revised and edited by Stewart Benedict, New York, Harper & Row, 1966.

LONG: J. H. Long, *Slips of Tongue and Pen*, New York, D. Appleton and Company, 1896.

OED: *The Oxford English Dictionary*, London, Oxford University Press, 1928.

OUD: *The Oxford Universal Dictionary on Historical Principles*, third edition, London, Oxford University Press, 1955.

PARTRIDGE: Eric Partridge, *Usage and Abusage*, Penguin Reference Books edition, Baltimore, Md., Penguin Books, 1963.

PARTRIDGE DS: Eric Partridge, *A Dictionary of Slang and Unconventional English*, fifth edition, New York, The Macmillan Company, 1961.

PENCE: R. W. Pence, *A Grammar of Present-Day English*, New York, The Macmillan Company, 1947.

RANDOM HOUSE: *The Random House Dictionary of the English Language*, New York, Random House, 1966.

WEBSTER II: *Webster's New International Dictionary of the English Language*, second edition, Springfield, Mass., G. & C. Merriam Company, 1959.

WEBSTER III: *Webster's Third New International Dictionary of the English Language*, Springfield, Mass., G. & C. Merriam Company, 1961.

WEBSTER'S NEW WORLD: *Webster's New World Dictionary of the American Language*, second college edition, Cleveland and New York, The World Publishing Company, 1970.

Acknowledgments of help are in order here. Bertram Lippman of the English Department of Bayside High

School, New York City, contributed greatly to the preparation of this book by providing advice, criticism and tireless research, all of it sound. If there is an item or two herein that he does not wholly agree with, it's because I am so stubborn. I am grateful also to Lewis Jordan, news editor of *The New York Times* and editor of its Style Book. He applied a sharp eye and a keen intellect to the task of editing this compilation, as he did earlier for *Watch Your Language* and *The Careful Writer*. He, too, may not agree with every item in these pages, but after all, who will? Leonard R. Harris, editor-publisher, supplied guidance and good counsel, as he did for three of my previous books. And then there are the uncounted correspondents who, through letters to me, unwittingly provided material for not a few of the book's entries. Obviously former pupils of Miss Thistlebottom, they directed my attention to bugbears I had either forgotten or never encountered. I am grateful to them, too, even though they may not in every instance reciprocate the sentiment.

T. M. B.

New York

Prologue

DEAR TED:

You may be wondering why I picked this time suddenly to take my pen in hand and write to you. You have not seen me and I have not seen you since your days at P.S. 10 when you were a little boy in my English class.

What prompts me to write now is the fact that I have been reading your book *The Careful Writer*. Many things in that book fill me with pride in you. I would be less than candid, however, if I did not say that the disparaging remarks you make about me in several places hurt me. Only Heaven knows why you felt it necessary to inject those comments. Was I really as hidebound and as rigid about rules of English as your remarks suggest? None of the data about me that you present is really favorable.

I do not know why I should be surprised at what you have written. Having had nothing but boys in my classes, I know perfectly well the truth of the nursery rhyme that describes of what little boys are made.

Despite all, however, I am of a forgiving nature and I am content with the thought that I must have taught you something right if you were able to turn out that book.

Yours sincerely,

BERTHA THISTLEBOTTOM

[3]

DEAR MISS THISTLEBOTTOM:

You can't do that to me. You can't suddenly write me a complaining letter after all I've done for you. Don't forget you are a character, not a person. I created you. You may be Miss Thistlebottom to yourself and others, but I have always thought of you as Myth Thistlebottom. You are not supposed to materialize abruptly and turn on me. It's as if Lady Sneerwell took it into her head to sue Sheridan for libel.

Don't think I have not noticed that your letter is cunningly calculated to win you public sympathy and to make me look like an ungrateful wretch. I don't know whether you are entitled to sympathy or not. But you are entitled to understanding and I mean to give you that. At the same time I mean to point out where I think you have gone wrong and how, in your efforts to keep your pupils upright in their English usage, you have sometimes bound them into a straitjacket.

Your letter has served one purpose anyway. It has opened a correspondence, and when I say correspondence I am deliberately misusing the word in a manner that you would not sanction. This correspondence is going to be completely one-sided; you will not get in a word edgewise. I intend to write you when the spirit moves me and you will not be able to talk back.

To make clear at once that I am willing to accord you understanding, I should say that I do not think for a moment that you alone are responsible for the many needless strictures, taboos and superstitions that have grown up around the use of the English language. Some writers, some book editors, some newspapermen have invented scarecrows, too, and I hope to introduce you to some of them as we go along.

But over the years teachers, in addition to making a priceless contribution to the preservation and flexibility of our language, have had a share in clamping some fetters on it. I think the fetters are a natural outgrowth of pedagogical training and of pedagogy itself. I trace it back to your student days at normal school (or was it already called teachers college when you went there?). By the way, to get off the subject a little, I was wondering why it was called "normal school" and I tried every dictionary I could find. It's hard to believe, but although every dictionary defined the term, I could not find one that explained why a normal school was called "normal." I finally ran the derivation down in William and Mary Morris's *Dictionary of Word and Phrase Origins*. According to the Morrises, the first of the teacher-training institutions was established in France in 1685 by the Brothers of the Christian Schools and such schools were called *école normale* because they were intended to establish a "norm" for all other schools.

But let me get back to the subject.

My surmise is that prospective teachers either are told explicitly or they apprehend implicitly that it is better to set rules for pupils than to put forth general principles that leave room for individual judgments in particular cases. Surely that would be reasonable, considering that school classes are composed of both eggheads and dunderheads. To take a concrete instance, it is probably more effective to tell a class never to split an infinitive than to say that sometimes it is all right to split an infinitive but normally it is not. Thus, almost everybody goes out into the world with a flat rule: Don't split infinitives. For the vast majority, whose writing does not extend beyond putting together a job application or composing a letter to Dad asking for a check, the rule will shield them against criticism. But for the rest, to whom writing is an art or a necessity (and the two are not mutually exclusive), the rule is too confining; it is like telling a driver, "Never go more than forty miles an hour."

As a pedagogical procedure this laying down of rules is understandable. Equally understandable is the laying down of rules by editors, many of whom are in a situation analagous to that of teachers in the sense that they often supervise staffs of men and women possessing talents almost as unequal as those of pupils in public schools. Sometimes, however, editors issue rules for what they think are good and sufficient reasons, but the rules turn out to be personal prejudices lacking a sound basis of usage or linguistic history. I should know because I did it myself some years back.

In reading a news dispatch I came across a sentence that said, "The French have an estimated 40,000 troops and police on hand to maintain order." I had read similar constructions hundreds of times and had thought nothing of them. But this time I was struck by the incongruity between the plural noun phrase "40,000 troops and police" and the singular article "an." "An 40,000 troops"? It hit me as grammatical nonsense. I thought—and I said semipublicly—that this kind of journalistic shorthand should properly be filled out to say "an estimated total of 40,000 troops and police." No one challenged that thought. Years later, however, I discovered a section in Otto Jespersen's A Modern English Grammar that discussed and accepted similar but not identical constructions. Almost all the examples Jespersen offered contained plural phrases that included elements considered as making up a single unit rather than considered severally—"a delightful three weeks," "a good three-quarters of a mile away," "another ten days," "a whole twenty pounds." Still there it was—approving recognition of the construction. My criticism of it must be set down as a personal prejudice. But I still don't like it and I would not write it myself. Other editors, I am afraid, have issued pronunciamentos with even less basis.

My recognition of my own prejudice and the consequent loosening of my rigidity on the subject is interesting in another way. The normal trend of human development is from liberalism, perhaps even radicalism, to conservatism. The youth is liberal, seeing justly that things need change and reform, but maturity brings the realization that all that is desirable is not possible and that what is possible may not after all be desirable. But in the field of usage the swing not infrequently is in just the opposite direction. Because of schoolbook rules and classroom assertion of authority, the tendency of youth—and I am speaking now of those who view the subject seriously—is toward a conservative rigidity about language. But as those who are closely involved with the language examine it more thoroughly and observe what usage does to slowly renovate it, they tend to give the rules a second look, their attitude becomes less frozen.

In matters of usage there are two extremes. At the extreme right are the purists, the standpatters, the rigid traditionalists who brook little or no change and who go by the rules—as many rules as they can recall or invent. They may not speak or write brilliantly, but they are grammatically unassailable—except when they forget some rule or misinterpret one. They owe everything to you, dear Miss Thistlebottom, but they could bill you for a few things, too. At the extreme left are the permissivists, the heretics who argue that there is no such thing as "correct" usage. They maintain that usage is what people say, but they neglect to disclose what people they are talking about—most people in general or most intelligent people or most educated people or most writing people or what. Oddly enough, despite the

loose approach of the permissivists, who have made some
headway in the schools, there is evidence that people do
crave authority in matters of language, they do ask for rules
and rulings. They do not seem to appreciate the freedom
that the permissivists are so eager to bestow upon them.
They do seem to want a middle way. And, of course, they
are right. As in so many other endeavors in life, in the use of
English an avoidance of extremes is the way to achievement
and excellence.

Those who seek authority do not require a discussion of
the extremists of the left. But they may require a discussion
of the false authority or the overreaching of authority on
the right. Perhaps they need a little more freedom than you
have given them, Miss Thistlebottom, and perhaps I can
help point the way.

Yours, etc.

Witchcraft in Words

DEAR MISS THISTLEBOTTOM:

Carrying out my promise to indulge in a one-sided correspondence, I would now like to have words with you. Words and the strange sorcery that has been visited upon many of them will form the subject of this letter. Not syntax, not idioms, not style—all of which I hope to take up with you in later letters—but just words.

Probably the most prolific source of word bogies is the stubborn notion that it is only the "original" meanings of words that can be permitted to exist. An editor of my acquaintance objected to using *ghetto* to describe urban Negro slums. I am certainly no radical when it comes to usage, but I made the point that although the word originally meant the Jewish quarter of a town, it had been justifiably extended to refer to any section in which a racial or national or religious group lives or to which it is restricted. Justifiably, because the word is appropriate and because there is no other single word that conveys the new meaning. Applying new meanings to old words is one of the ways in which the language is kept viable and adequate to its tasks. Usually we notice changes in meanings only when they occur within our own lifetimes. We are not aware that such changes occurred far back in many words that we don't give a second thought to today. It would not be known to most of us that a simple word like *nice* began with the meaning of foolish or stupid and has since undergone perhaps half a dozen mutations. Or that a more complicated word like

[9]

sophisticated in its early stages meant such things as wise, adulterated and corrupted. Sometimes, of course, the changes arise from ignorance, but the fact that the ignorant usage catches on and hangs on indicates that it is filling some need, large or small.

Occasionally such a need is supplied by the coinage of a new word. And that, too, often meets head-on resistance. When convicts were first put to death in the electric chair, the word *electrocute,* combining the ideas of *electric* and *execute,* came into being, but instantly and persistently it encountered hostility, which was overcome only after the passing of many decades. There can be no doubt, however, that new things frequently require new words to describe them. In this age of startling scientific developments we have grown somewhat more accustomed to the advent of such terms.

Still another bugbear arises whenever common usage employs a word as a different part of speech from the one we are accustomed to. *Above* and *following* are now frequently used as nouns whereas they previously were adjectives, and there has been a great deal of hubbub about that development. (*See* ABOVE.) But such conversions are not unusual: In medicine we have *prophylactics* and *sedatives,* in military life we have *privates, regulars* and *offensives,* and more recently in broadcasting we have *documentaries, visuals* and *specials.* The list could go on and on. Nor would it be confined to the conversion of adjectives into nouns. It is just as common to find nouns doing duty as adjectives, beginning with such inconspicuous ones as *rail road* and *stock yard* and going on to *population explosion* and *atom bomb agreement.* The conversions are not always felicitous, but they cannot be forbidden as a class.

And then there are the attacks on words that seem to have been dreamed up by people suffering from insomnia.

(Don't ask me how insomniacs can dream, but if they can invent such attacks on words, they are capable of anything.) I am thinking here of such objections as the ones raised against *all-time* and *bipartisan*, which you will find in the appended list. Those objections can only be devised by trouble-trackers—people intent on making mischief.

Now that I have mentioned the appended list, Miss Thistlebottom, why don't I just append it? The words speak for themselves. And that is what words are supposed to do.

Yours, etc.

ABOVE

Many teachers have adjured their charges to avoid the use of *above* in such phrases as "the statement appearing above," "the above statement," "the above-mentioned statement" and "the above is a definitive statement." Obviously they were not giving vent to personal prejudices because purists have long been condemning such employment of the word. Indeed, Partridge comes out with a flat command, "Avoid it," followed by a terrifying exclamation point. Nevertheless, the preponderance of evidence is that those various uses of *above* are quite legitimate and aboveboard. The revised Fowler says: "There is ample authority, going back several centuries, for this use of *above* as adverb, adjective or noun, and no solid ground for the pedantic criticism of it sometimes heard."

Grammatical criticisms aside, however, a valid objection is made against such uses of *above*: that they convey a legalistic or commercial flavor, which is inappropriate in normal prose. That is unquestionably true, just as it is true that *said, aforesaid* and *the same* convey a similar flavor. I have an additional objection, which may or may not be peculiar to me. Unless you are reading the original manuscript of the Declaration of Independence, there is a fifty-fifty chance that a reference to something *above* will be an incorrect statement; it is not unlikely that you will be reading at the top of a page and the something *above* will prove to be below, at the bottom of the preceding page. But perhaps I am being literal rather than literary.

ABSOLUTES   *See* INCOMPARABLES.

ACCUSED *See* ALLEGED.

ADMINISTER

Here we have another attempt by the driven-snow purists to restrict a word to its primary meaning. *Administer* means, to be sure, to manage or direct or superintend, but it also means, and for a long time has meant, other things, too. The Cowles book tells us not to use it in the sense of to deal, as in to administer blows. But Webster II says it means to give and, by extension, is used of a blow, a reproof or the like. What more is needed to administer a fatal blow to those purists?

ADVERBS

It is true that "-ly" is used to make adverbs out of adjectives (*gladly*), participles (*lovingly*) and sometimes nouns (*totally*). That does not mean, however, that to be an adverb a word must end in "-ly," as is believed by those who are irritated by signs that read, "Go slow." Nor is the use of *slow* as an adverb a recent innovation; the OED dates it back as far as 1500. Like *slow*, many other adverbs have two forms. There are, for example, *bad, badly; bright, brightly; cheap, cheaply; clear, clearly; close, closely; even, evenly; fair, fairly; hard, hardly; high, highly; late, lately; loud, loudly; right, rightly; sharp, sharply; tight, tightly; wrong, wrongly*. It should be noted that although the words of some of these sets can be used interchangeably—"go slow" or "go slowly"—others cannot be so used. We cannot say, for instance, "The defendant was wrong imprisoned." When there is a real choice and idiom does not require one form or the other, the tendency in reputable writing is to use the "-ly" version.

ADVISEDLY

Bierce frowned on this word as a synonym for *advertently* or *intentionally*, observing that " 'It was done advisedly' should mean that it was done after advice." Nothing of the kind. Anyway, very little of the kind. The notions in the words *advice* and *advised* are quite different, though the words are not unrelated etymologically. *Advice* and *advise*, of course, have to do with the giving of counsel, but *advised* and *advisedly* have to do—and for centuries have had to do—with deliberation, careful consideration. *Advice* is something you get from outside, but when you are *well-advised* or *ill-advised* or when you do something *advisedly* your counsel is self-contained.

ALIBI

Hands have been wrung over the latter-day secondary meaning that has been attached to *alibi*. In its original meaning it is a legal term denoting a plea that an accused person was elsewhere than at the scene of the crime when the offense was committed. Its newer meaning refers to an excuse, often an invented excuse, to shift responsibility. The hand-wringers suppose that it is merely a synonym for *excuse*, but it is more than that. It carries a connotation of slight or outright dishonesty and it represents a plea to get out from under. It is not, therefore, a pretentious and needless synonym, but rather a useful word with its own peculiar meaning. If it were likely that the newer meaning would drive the original one into oblivion, the complainers would have a case. The revised Fowler fears just that contingency: "The mischief is that, if this goes on, we shall be left without a word for the true meaning of *alibi*." There is no reason to believe, however, that such a situation will come to pass. Lawyers and the courts continue to use the word in its juridical meaning, the press continues to repo.

it in that sense and the public continues to understand it in the legal context. We may with some confidence expect that the two meanings will coexist amicably.

ALLEGED

Necessity is the mother of invention, and the journalistic use of *alleged* comes right out of the womb of necessity. Bierce quite rightly objected to such phrases as "the alleged murderer," saying: "One can allege a murder, but not a murderer; a crime, but not a criminal." Nevertheless, newspapers, in the interest of fairness, do not wish to state anything beyond what they know to be the fact, and, in their own self-interest, wish to set up some kind of protection, no matter how flimsy, in any legal action that might result from their characterization of a defendant. Therefore they introduce *alleged* as a softener. It is quite true that the word is no defense against a charge of libel. But it could be used to demonstrate an absence of malice and thus reduce or eliminate damages. Bierce recognized this reason for the use of the word and he was aware of the lack of any other single word that expresses the desired meaning, but he objected to the word nonetheless and suggested getting around it. Although such an evasion might be possible in the text of a news story, it is not usually feasible in a cramped headline. In any event, the word has been so widely and frequently used that it is recognized in all the newest dictionaries.

Two other words whose meanings have been similarly distorted are *accused* and *suspected*. An "accused spy" is not, of course, a spy who has been accused, as the words would suggest, but a person accused as a spy; a "suspected robber" is not a robber who is under suspicion but a person suspected of being a robber. But these journalistic uses of the adjectives are also now accepted, though because of their ambiguity it would be better to avoid them.

ALLEGEDLY, REPORTEDLY

Newsmen could hardly get along without these words, but Follett could. He finds them lacking in the characteristics of a respectable adverb and adds that in general adverbs made by adding "-ly" to past participles are deplorable. Then he sets forth a formula: "The test of legitimacy for an adverb made from an adjective is that it fit the formula *in (x) manner*. Thus *wisely* = in a wise manner; *forbiddingly* = in a forbidding manner." Naturally, on the basis of this formula *allegedly* or *reportedly* will not wash. "In an alleged manner"? "In a reported manner"? No. But plenty of other natural English adverbs could not meet so strict a test: *admittedly, formerly, mostly, hardly, presently, previously, recently, repeatedly, reputedly, shortly, supposedly.* The trouble is that the test is too narrow and too rigid. Although the "-ly" suffix does in general denote "in (x) manner," that does not mean that those words must be used literally in defining the adverb. However, leaving etymology aside, we may observe that *allegedly, reportedly* and many other adverbs formed by adding "-ly" to past participles are recognized parts of the language and often quite useful parts. Especially to newsmen.

ALL-TIME

An editor of my acquaintance used to object to the term *all-time* in such a sentence as this: "The volume of trading on the Stock Exchange yesterday set an all-time high." His objection, if I understood him correctly, was that *all-time* includes the past, the present and the future and that of the future we can know nothing. It always seemed to me that if the argument against the word was to be presented in those philosophic terms, the answer might well be in equally philosophic terms: We do not know for sure that there is going to be any future and time can be reckoned only up to the present second; therefore, *all-time* refers only to the past up to the knowable present second. That, indeed, is what a writer means by *all-time*. The additional argument was advanced, if my recollection still serves, that when a writer spoke of "an all-time high," all he really meant was a record and he should say just that. The trouble with that contention is that the word *record* often needs qualification. There are records for the current month or the current year, for the past decade or for the first Tuesday of the month provided there is a full moon. *All-time* is perfectly acceptable provided it is not superfluous, as it is in a sentence such as this: "Jones set an all-time pro-football record for completed passes in one season."

ALMOST *See* NEARLY, ALMOST.

ALONE, ONLY

The Cowles book declares that *alone* means unaccompanied and *only* means there is no other. The implication is that that is that. The book gives the examples "He suffered alone" (no one with him) and "Only he suffered" (no other person), as if to say that *alone* cannot be used as a synonym for *only*. That is incorrect. *Alone* can indeed be used to mean *only*, and an interesting fact is that word order, so important in English, can often determine when the use is proper. Let's work the variations on the Cowles three-word example:

> *Alone, he suffered* = *all by himself*
> *He suffered alone* = *all by himself*
> *He alone suffered* = *and nobody else*

There is nothing esoteric about this demonstration; anyone who is familiar with English instantly recognizes the different meaning that is conveyed by the variation in word order. And the conclusion here is that *alone* can in fact be used as a synonym for *only*.

ALTERNATIVES

Purists point to the Latin *alter*, meaning other (of two), from which *alternatives* is derived, and insist that the word can apply only to a choice between two possibilities. That position, says Fowler, is a "fetish." The word has been used reputably to apply to more than two possibilities since at least the middle of the nineteenth century. Who are we to dishonor our forefathers?

AMERICA, AMERICAN

It is unquestionably true that *America* takes in a great deal more territory than just the United States and it is also true that technically *American* should apply to Indians and Peruvians as well as to citizens of the United States. All of which does not alter the irreversible fact that in usage *America* means the United States and *American* means either one of its citizens or pertaining to that country. As far as the adjective is concerned, there is no word that refers exclusively to the United States. It's not a matter of presumptuousness; it's rather a linguistic fact of life.

ANYPLACE, SOMEPLACE

No, a blessing will not be put on these words here. In Great Britain they are definitely disapproved; in the United States they are accepted in spoken English, but not fully accepted in good written English. But if so reputable a writer as Edmund Wilson has used *anyplace*, as Webster III says he has, the graffito is clearly evident. The objection to these words seems to be that a noun, *place*, is being used as if it were an adverb. No objection is raised, however, to a similar use in such phrases as "no placc to hide" and "a place to live." Other nouns have been used acceptably with adverbial force and it is quite possible that in a couple of decades *anyplace* and *someplace* will not provoke the slightest grimace. Let it be noted also that "I'd like to go to some place warm" is acceptable because the noun is being used properly as a noun, governed by a preposition.

APPRECIATE

In its primary meaning *appreciate*, used transitively, means to evaluate truly. Bierce says it does not mean to evaluate highly. Follett says it is too late to try to hold the word to its primary meaning, but grows sadly wistful about its expansion. Follett is nearer the truth than Bierce. The word has come to mean more than merely to evaluate justly; it connotes to esteem highly or even to be grateful for. So if someone says, "I appreciate your ability," accept it modestly as a compliment and don't try to correct his English.

AQUACADE *See* CAVALCADE.

AT, BY

This is another Bierce-ism. Under the heading "At for By," the following appears: " 'She was shocked at his conduct.' This very common solecism is without excuse." And so, one might add, is the designation of that use as a solecism. Webster II offers as one meaning of *at*, this definition: "Indicating a relation of source, cause, or occasion." It then presents as an example: ". . . surprised or angry *at* this rudeness." And Webster's New World gives the meaning "because of: as, terrified *at* the sight." All this is not to say that *at* and *by* are always interchangeable. We may be surprised *at* Bierce's position, but we should not be cowed or intimidated *at* (x) him.

AUDIENCE

Literally an *audience* is a group of listeners, and in most instances it is well to be literal about the word. But there are, and should be, exceptions. Those in attendance at a pantomime show or a circus or a silent movie can also be called an *audience* and no one can validly object. However, we should not speak of an *audience* at a sports event or at the scene of an airplane crash. On the other hand, is there an *audience* for this book?

BACK FORMATIONS

If you were to start with the word *prognosis* and decide that it must be derived from an actual word, in the same way that *analysis* is derived from *analyze,* and then you were to come up with the verb *prognose,* you would be indulging in back formation and the word you had coined would be a back formation. A back formation is a word invented in the erroneous belief that an actual existing word is derived from it. You would expect—and there are those who would contend—that such coinages must be outlawed because they are too ridiculous for words.

Examine, however, the perfectly acceptable word *diagnose.* It came into existence in 1861 in precisely the way that *prognose* was devised in the foregoing fanciful example. Since it served a useful purpose, it has won its way into respectable usage. There are many others like that: *scavenge, grovel, laze, peddle, drowse.* Other back formations linger in an indeterminate state between reluctant and full acceptance: *enthuse, commentate.* Still others are purely jocular or otherwise not yet acceptable: *burgle, emote, gruntled, butle.*

One cannot rule out back formations as such. Much depends on whether there is a genuine need for them and whether reputable users of the language employ them.

BALANCE

Some purists who seem to think that the primary literal meaning of a word is the only acceptable one rule out the use of *balance* in the sense of remainder or rest. This is too rigid an attitude. The bookkeeping term may be legitimately extended when there is a real parallel to bookkeeping—that is, when two amounts are involved. Thus, it is acceptable to say, "Of the $150,000,000 appropriation, $100,000,000 will go for school construction and the balance for salaries." It is not entirely acceptable, however, to say, "The pupils were excused for the balance of the day."

BANQUET

Most newspaper editors recoil in horror if a reporter writes about a *banquet* given by the Volunteer Firemen's Battalion of East Dudsville. And they are right to do so. The frozen pizza pie main course, the dreary beer and the drearier speeches by the Captain and the Head Selectman do not qualify such an occasion as a banquet. That does not mean, however, that the word must never, never be used. True enough, it is most properly applied to a gala, sumptuous feast of food and drink accompanied by elaborate entertainment, speeches and ceremony. But these days the sumptuousness of the food and drink is less important than it once was, so that if the occasion is elaborate enough, the fact that the entree is embalmed chicken might not disqualify the affair. A four-course dinner in a prestigious hotel at-

tended by the Governor and at least one Councilman
(there will probably be more if the Governor is there)
might rank as a *banquet*. The word should not be ruled out.
But in general the editors are right.

BET, BETTED

If Bierce had had his way, the past tense of *bet* would
always be *betted*. He would also have had us use the "-ed"
past tense for *wet, wed, quit* and "others that are misconjugated." He has not had his way in any of these instances
and is not likely to have. Americans often seem to prefer
short forms when there is a choice, and *bet* as the past tense
is far more common—and just as valid—as *betted*. (*But see*
FIT, FITTED.)

BETWEEN

Grammar teachers have long been insistent that *between*
should be used only when two elements are involved and
that if more than two are involved the preposition should
be *among*. By and large and for the purposes of the great
majority of pupils that position was correct. Indeed, the
very derivation of the word suggests that the "two" idea is
inherent in it: The "tween" has a kinship to the word
"twain." But just between you and me and the lamppost,
exceptions to the rule should be noted.

What the careful writer must ask himself is not how
many elements are involved but rather what is the relationship they bear to one another. If the relationship involves
sets of two, the word *between* is appropriate, no matter how
many elements are involved. For instance, it is proper to
speak of a treaty *between* the four powers that have nuclear
weapons because the treaty binds every power to each of the
three others. *Among* would not be improper, but it is a
vaguer, more general word. Likewise it would be proper to

say that a triangular plot of land lies *between* three points and not entirely proper to say it lies *among* three points. As another example, there is a helicopter service *between* (not *among*) Kennedy, La Guardia and Newark Airports. And a speaker could quite correctly say to two companions, "Let's keep this a secret *between* ourselves," meaning, if you want to analyze it, between himself and A, between himself and B and between A and B.

BIPARTISAN

One editor I know objects to a sentence such as this: "Legislation to keep the dinosaur extinct has bipartisan support." His point is that *partisan* means something like blindly favorable to a cause and that therefore *bipartisan* must mean the same kind of unreasoning devotion to a cause by two parties. His premise is correct, but his conclusion is faulty, because the meaning of *partisan* changes when it acquires the prefix. Perhaps this does not seem logical, but it is the fact. *Bipartisan* means merely representative of two sides. If he prefers the word *bipartite*, he is at liberty to use it, but he must not censure the rest of us for using *bipartisan*.

BIRTHDAY

This is another journalistic superstition: the notion that a person can have only one *birthday*, namely, the day on which he is born. Those gripped by the superstition insist that a subsequent recurrence of the date must be called a *birthday anniversary*. Utter nonsense. *Birthday* has meant either the actual day of birth or an anniversary of that day just about as long as the word has been in existence.

BOGUS

The objection to *bogus*, meaning spurious or counterfeit,

is that the word is slang. It was indeed a cant word when it first cropped up in the United States a century and a half ago, but it has since won its way into reputable usage. As a noun it is printers' jargon referring to type that duplicates material already in printable form and that is set in a newspaper composing room only because of a union rule. *See also* FAKE.

BUGGER
Originally a low word meaning a person who commits sodomy, *bugger* is now an acceptable term used humorously or even affectionately to describe a fellow, a chap, a guy. The original coarse meaning has either been forgotten by or is not known to users of the word, just as the origins of *nuts, bollix* and *jerk* have largely faded into obscurity.

BURGLARIZE
Although some dictionaries label *burglarize* colloquial, they very likely will not continue to do so for long. The reason is that the word fills a need; there is no other way to describe the action short of a cumbersome phrase such as "break into to commit theft." On the other hand, with *burglarize* well on its way to acceptability, the verb *burgle*, a back formation from *burglar*, will undoubtedly continue to be labeled colloquial and humorous. Who needs it?

CAVALCADE
Undoubtedly there are those who, because they know that the root of *cavalcade* is a word meaning horse, would restrict the term to a procession on horseback. But they are too literal. Now that horses have become rare outside of racetracks, the word has, in a way, outlived them; it is applied to any ceremonial procession.
Oddly enough, folk etymologists apparently thought the

"-cade" part of the word meant a procession and so they then came up with the word *motorcade*, meaning a procession of automobiles. Proceeding from that point, other folk etymologists coined the word *aquacade*, which, though not exactly a procession of swimmers, was an exhibition by swimmers. The first thing you know, someone is going to decide that a procession of ten years is a *decade*.

CHOMP

If a newspaper reporter interviews a cigar-smoking subject, the chances are that at some point in his story he will have the subject *chomping* on his cigar. When the word appeared in one newspaper in two proximate stories on a single day, a reader wrote to the editor asking whether people didn't ever just puff on their cigars and saying that he could not find the word *chomp* in his desk dictionary. The word does appear in five larger dictionaries, but only grudgingly; in each instance it is dismissed as a variant of *champ*. In a way this is odd. The word is undoubtedly a variant of *champ*, but by giving it the backs of their hands the dictionaries suggest that it is uncommon and that *champ* is the normal and dominant word. True enough, a horse (as well as an impatient person) *"champs* at the bit," but once you have said that you have just about exhausted the uses of *champ*. No one ever *champs* on a cigar or on his walnuts or on his well-done toast. Nor does he *chump* on it—five dictionaries give that as another variant. The dominant word these days is *chomp*. And the suspicion is strong that the dictionaries have been looking over one another's shoulders.

CLIPPED WORDS

As time-savers and breath-savers, clipped words defy the pedants and win their way to respectability. This has been true for a long time—witness *piano* from *pianoforte* and *cello* from *violoncello*—and it is even truer today when technical words seem to grow longer and more complicated and the patience of speakers grows shorter—witness *strep* for *streptococcus* and *recap* for *recapitulation*. Thus, anyone who tries to battle against *phone, taxi, cab, auto, plane* or *copter* may be assured that he is waging a losing fight.

CONGRESSMAN

On many newspapers the use of *Congressman* to denote a member of the lower house in Washington is verboten. It is true that dictionaries are just about unanimous in defining the word as "a member of Congress" (or "a congress"), but they are also unanimous in going on to say "especially of the House of Representatives." The fact is that although a Senator is a member of Congress, no one would dream of referring to him as a *Congressman*, and still less would one do so in his waking moments. Therefore, *Representative* may be a trifle more precise, but *Congressman* is wholly acceptable.

CONTACT

As a verb meaning to communicate with, *contact* has drawn objections from conservatives. The only ground on which valid objection can be registered to it is that it is an overworked fad word. But it is by no means unusual for a noun to be verbed. Moreover, the word is often useful either because it replaces a longer locution, such as "get in touch with" (which, by the way, is precisely what *contact* means), or because it is intentionally less specific than some other word such as *phone, write, call on, meet* or *find*. The objectors to *contact* are fighting a losing battle and may as well surrender.

COUPLE OF

Using *a couple of* in the indefinite sense of a few or several is frowned upon by judges of reputable writing; dictionaries tend to label it "informal." But that does not rule out the use of the phrase in the exact sense of two, as in "A *couple of* horses were nuzzling each other in the pasture." Let it be noted also that what is definitely substandard is the omission of the word "of" in the phrase. You cannot say "a couple horses" and retain the esteem of your cultivated fellows.

CREATE

"Only God can create something," an old-time editor must have told his intimidated hirelings, some of whom went through the country spreading that gospel. The linguistic fact is, however, that to anyone but the most fundamentalist zealot *create* means simply to originate or bring into being and it is something that can be done by mortal man.

CRITICIZE

It is true that criticism does not necessarily entail an adverse appraisal. That is especially true when one is speaking about criticism of plays, paintings or books. Still a coordinate meaning of *criticize* is to appraise unfavorably or to censure, and that is by far the more common meaning. If we talk about criticism of a play, the judgment could go either way, but if we talk about criticism of the school system, we are thinking of disapproval; if we speak of critics of the arts, we are referring to appraisers, but if we speak of critics of the Administration, we are referring to disparagers.

CULMINATE

One book on usage says that the use of *culminate* as a

transitive verb is "a popular error," adding that the word is an intransitive verb only. That dictum would rule out such a sentence as, "His election culminated six months of strenuous campaigning." Although the OUD calls the transitive use rare, that use is nothing newfangled; it dates back to 1659. Virtually all other dictionaries find it completely acceptable and so do hosts of skilled writers.

CULTURED, CULTIVATED

There are those who tend to imagine a distinction between words where none exists or where the distinction is so minute as to defy definition. People who ask about the difference between *somebody* and *someone* fall into that category. And so do those—and there are a few—who inquire about the difference between *cultured* and *cultivated*. Both words pertain to urbanity, development of the intellect and aesthetic appreciation. It may be that *cultivated* contains a faint connotation of the process by which culture is achieved, but for all practical purposes the two words mean the same thing.

DECIMATE

The original meaning of *decimate* was to kill one in ten and it referred to the punishment meted out to Roman legions for cowardice or mutiny whereby those to be put to death were chosen by lot. About the same proportion of present-day users of the language take one look at that "deci-" prefix and decide that the word simply must refer to one-tenth or it is being misused. Such insistence is no more valid than to demand that *testify* be used only where there is some reference to the testicles. Actually the broader use of *decimate* to mean the destroying of a large part dates back to the mid 1600's and is completely reputable. The only thing to guard against is employing the word in connection with some other numerical proportion, as in this ridiculous sentence: "Half the corn crop was *decimated* by parasites."

DEMEAN

Sentries at the door of the empty barn would have us restrict *demean* to the sense of to behave or comport (oneself). But the use of the word in the sense of to debase or degrade is far more common than the other one and established its credentials as far back as the start of the seventeenth century. Most likely the secondary meaning arose from a mistaking of the "-mean" part as denoting lowness and the drawing of an analogy with *debase*, or perhaps from confusion with *bemean*. But whatever the origin, the horse is now out of the barn and thriving in green pastures.

DICTION

The principal meaning of *diction* is the selection and use of words or the manner of expression. But this fact does not rule out, as some purists would like to do, the companion meaning of mode of speaking or enunciation. Indeed, since the word traces back to a Latin root meaning to say, the companion definition is obviously legitimate and it is well established.

DIPLOMAT, DIPLOMATIST

Diplomat has always been the preferred form in the United States in referring to one skilled in or engaging in diplomacy. In Britain, however, *diplomatist* was, until fairly recently, the more common version, and Anglophiles did their damnedest to foist it on their fellow Yankees. The trend of things is reflected in Fowler's *Modern English Usage*. The original text said: "The longer English formation is preferable to the un-English -*mat*. . . ." The second

edition, revised by Sir Ernest Gowers and published in
1965, says: "The shorter formation, standard in U.S., is in-
creasingly used in Britain." First thing you know, they'll be
drinking bourbon in London.

DONATE

A back formation from *donation*, the verb *donate* reared
its ugly head in the nineteenth century as a formal synonym
for *give*. Ayres branded it an abomination, and other authorities denounced it. Still it has survived and won recognition. It is primarily an Americanism, but it is used to
some extent in Britain, too. Although one may reasonably
ask, "Why not use *give* or *grant* or *bestow* or *present?*" one
may not reasonably say, "Don't use *donate.*" It may be
noted, moreover, that in at least one context none of those
synonyms will do: An actor, for example, *donates* his serv-
ices at a charity performance; he doesn't *give* them or *grant*
them or anything else. See BACK FORMATIONS.

DOUBLE ENTENDRE

What some pseudoscholars, learned in French, if not in
English, would wish us to say is *double entente*. That, however, is ancient French and the modern English phrase—
modern, that is, since the seventeenth century—is *double
entendre*, signifying a double meaning, one sense of which
is slightly blue.

DOUBT

Some authorities, including Fowler and Gowers, maintain that when the verb *doubt* is used it should be followed
in an affirmative sentence by *whether* or *if* ("The doctor
doubted whether the patient would live") and in a negative
sentence by *that* or *but that* ("The doctor did not *doubt
that* the case was hopeless"). With the second precept

there is no argument. The first, concerning affirmative sentences, is subject to at least one exception, however. In affirmative statements *that* may be used when the intention is to express unbelief rather than a kind of negative uncertainty of opinion. Uncertainty: "He *doubted whether* the bill would be passed." Unbelief: "He *doubted that* the bill would be passed."

DURING

James Gordon Bennett cautioned his reporters and editors not to use *during* for *in* because "*during* means throughout the continuance of." That caution has been long-lived enough so that you will still hear it in a few newspaper offices. Bennett's definition is, to be sure, the original meaning of the word, but modern dictionaries give the additional meaning of at some time in the course of. *During* is not only proper but indeed preferable to *in* when used in such a sentence as, "We played tennis twice *during* our stay at the resort."

-ED

Is it a *four-engined plane* or a *four-engine plane?* Is it a *teen-aged girl* or a *teen-age girl?* If any observer of English usage besides me has been bothered by this problem, I have seen no evidence of it, and quite honestly I see no reason why anyone should be bothered by it. Nevertheless, it is a safe bet that at some time in the near or distant future someone will uncover a bugaboo about it.

There seem to be no rules about when to use or not use the "-ed" ending; it is a matter of, shall we say, idiom. In the questions posed above, either form is correct, and that is true of a good many compounds. However, most nouns formed into adjectives take the "-ed." But there are some that never do: *loose-leaf, paperback, three-ring, five-room.*

If there is anything even approximating a rule that can be set forth, it is that a nounal adjective describing a characteristic of an animate creature in most instances ends in "-ed." Thus we have a *left-handed man*, a *yellow-bellied sapsucker*, a *grim-faced statesman*, and a *floppy-eared dog*. It is true that we also have a *barefoot boy*, but despite that Whittier, but not necessarily better, phrase, *barefooted* is just about as common. We also speak of a *bareback rider*, but that phrase does not describe a personal characteristic of the rider; it's not his back that is bare, but the horse's. And anyone who says otherwise is a barefaced liar.

EITHER

In the sense of each of two, *either* has been criticized by some authorities. The original Fowler, for example, says: "The sense 'each of the two' as in 'the room has a fireplace at e. end,' is archaic & should be avoided except in verse or in special contexts." Gowers, who later revised and updated Fowler, says in his own *Complete Plain Words* that there does not seem to be any good ground for Fowler's dictum. As a matter of fact, the meaning each of two was the original one in Old English, as Fowler undoubtedly knew since he classed it as archaic. That it was the original sense should not invalidate it; indeed, it should reinforce the fact that it is still in wide and reputable use to make the meaning completely acceptable.

ELECTROCUTE

Both Bierce and Fowler were almost made ill by *electrocute*. Said Ambrose: "To one having even an elementary knowledge of Latin grammar this word is no less than disgusting, and the thing meant by it is felt to be altogether too good for the word's inventor." Said Henry: "This barbarism jars the unhappy latinist's nerves much more

cruelly than the operation denoted jars those of its victim."
The word may be tainted by bastardy when viewed as a
Latin derivation, but it is legitimate as a centaur word
blending *electricity* and *execute.* When Sir Ernest Gowers
got around to revising and updating Fowler he recognized
this and said that "as it is established, protest is idle." It
became established, of course, because when the New York
State Legislature approved this form of carrying out the
death penalty in 1888 and when the method was first put to
use at Auburn state prison in 1890 there was no other word
to describe it. And no substitute has come forward since.
Fortunately, as things are going these days both the word
and the operation it denotes seem destined to become obsolete. But there will always be accidental *electrocutions,* of
course.

ELLIPSIZE

In the entry headed THE (as in "Motherwell, the
painter") in the Spooks of Style section there is a footnote
directing the reader to this entry. Whether you arrived here
as a result of that direction or whether you just chanced on
this page, let it be confessed at once that there is no such
word as *ellipsize,* so that its appearance here provides an
opening for another taboo by the witches who distill such
taboos. But how the language has survived all these centuries without a verb denoting the creation of a grammatical
ellipsis staggers the imagination. As was noted in the entry
mentioned, when you speak of "Motherwell, the painter,"
you are *ellipsizing* "famous" or "noted" or some other such
word. It won't do to let the guardians of the language say,
"Why *ellipsizing?* You are *omitting* the word." But *omit*
usually has the connotation of deliberately not including
something. In ellipsis, however, there is no deliberation or
intention. When you say, "The girl I love," you are not de-

liberately or intentionally dropping "whom" after "girl."
When you write, "Three persons were killed and two injured," you are not deliberately or intentionally not insert-
ing "were" after "two." Nor does anyone in either instance
expect you to insert those words. In most such instances the
missing words do not even enter the mind of either the
writer or the reader. Therefore, the words have not been
omitted; they have rather not been inserted. In short, they
have been *ellipsized*.

ENGINEER

Engineers are rather touchy about the indiscriminate use
of their professional designation—and not without cause.
In an age in which we have *insurance engineers, bakery engineers, plumbing engineers* and maybe, for all anyone
knows, *hot dog engineers,* the gentlemen who take prescribed courses and are awarded licenses have a legitimate
complaint. But occasionally the complaints are illegitimate,
as, for example, an objection to calling the man who runs a
railroad locomotive an engineer. In this country that fellow
has been termed an *engineer* since at least 1839. In Britain,
of course, he is an *engine driver*, but there, as well as here,
the man who manages a ship's engines is an *engineer*.

ET CETERA

On the off chance that some present-day reader may have
come into possession of a little book called "Slips of
Tongue and Pen," by J. H. Long, M.A., LL.B., published in
1896, a word should be said about *et cetera* and its abbrevia-
tion *etc.* Mr. Long says that "*Etc.* means 'and others of a
different kind'" and he goes on to contrast it with *and so
forth*, which, he says, means "and others of the same kind."
In so saying Mr. Long has made a slip of either tongue or

pen. The truth is that *etc.* connotes "and others of the same kind."

There are three things about *etc.* that authorities on usage are agreed upon. One is that it is not appropriate to any kind of literary writing. A second is that it should not be used if a "such as" precedes it, since it then introduces a redundancy. A third is that it should not be preceded by *and* because the *et* means just that.

EVE

In its strict meaning, *eve* denotes the evening or the day before a holiday or some other special day, and there are strict people, including some editors, who would confine the word to that meaning. But, as is true of so many other words, this one may be used in a metaphorical as well as a literal sense. The only limitation is the need for discretion in employing the figurative meaning. If schools are scheduled to open on Sept. 7 and the teachers on Sept. 6 threaten a strike, it is of course proper to write, "On the eve of the opening of the schools the teachers threatened a strike." That is an instance of the literal use of the word. However, if the teachers on Aug. 10 threaten that strike, the sentence would not be proper, because the word could not be taken literally, nor could it be taken figuratively since the context is too commonplace, too matter-of-fact, to support a metaphor. On the other hand, in writing about the signing of the Soviet-Nazi nonaggression treaty on Aug. 24, 1939, preceding the beginning of World War II on Sept. 1, it would not be inappropriate to say, "On the eve of the outbreak of the war the Soviet Union and Nazi Germany signed a nonaggression treaty." Obviously no flat rule is possible for determining when the figurative use is proper and when it is not. In general the main event should be large enough—not

necessarily world-shaking, for it could be a birth or a death
—to warrant metaphorical treatment.

EVERYPLACE *See* ANYPLACE, SOMEPLACE.

EX-

Some editors used to command their headline writers to
attach the prefix *ex-* only to the principal noun in a phrase
of two or more words. Thus they would have to write
"Army Ex-Captain" or "British Ex-Official." Perhaps this
bugaboo derived from Fowler, where it is written in the
original edition, "the ex-Tory Solicitor-General for Scot-
land (i.e. the Solicitor-General who formerly was but no
longer is a Tory)," and in the revised edition, "Ex-Prime
Minister suggests a minister who is past his prime." To say
that it takes a deal of perversity to derive those meanings
from the hyphenated phrases is not to deny that they are a
wee bit awkward. But the solution is not the one decreed by
those editors; otherwise the first thing you know we will be
reading about a "lightweight ex-champion" or a "female ex-
impersonator." The difficulty in either version lies in the
illogicality of coupling the *ex-* to the part when the intention is to couple it to the whole. Of the two choices the
preferable one is to put the *ex-* at the head of the phrase.
That advice is addressed to headline writers. For the rest of
us the best course is to change *ex-* to *former*.

EXECUTE

One school of thought (if that is the right word) didn't
like the use of *execute* to mean put to death. The contention
was that it is the sentence that is *executed*, not the man. It
is true that *execute* originally meant—and in one of its defi-
nitions still means—to carry out, to put into effect. Yet in
the sense of put to death, *execute* was in use, though rare,

according to the OED, as far back as 1483. Today that is a principal meaning of the word.

EXECUTIVE

A letter writer asserts that an *executive* is one who makes policy and has the authority in an organization to see that it is carried out. Everyone else, says he, is an *administrator*, a *supervisor* or something else. That may be true in his organization, but it is not generally true. The word is from a Latin root meaning to follow out or put into effect; therefore an *executive*, strictly speaking, is one who executes or puts into effect a policy or program, although he may also have something to do with framing it. Anyhow, in the business usage of today an *executive* seems to be anyone above the level of office boy.

EYEWITNESS

Undoubtedly in ninety-nine cases out of a hundred a witness to an occurrence is someone who has seen it. Therefore, some editors have said, *eyewitness* is a redundant word and it should be consigned to the dustbin. But hold; let us not be too precipitate in the dumping process. To begin with, there are such things as "earwitnesses." In addition, there are in legal cases witnesses whose testimony concerns neither what they saw nor what they heard. Therefore, there is sometimes need to specify *eyewitness*. Frowning on the word is a species of nit-picking.

FAIL

It is true that fail should not be used to express a mere "not" idea as in "He failed to enjoy his dinner" or in "The Soviet Union has failed to cross the border for fear of touching off a nuclear war." It is not true, however, to assert, as one writer does, that "failure carries always the sense of endeavor; when there has been no endeavor there is no failure." That narrows the meaning of the word far too much. In addition to presupposing a goal or an intention, *fail* also may presuppose a requirement or an expectation. Thus it is perfectly proper to write, "The sentry *failed* to sound an alarm" or "He was scheduled to speak at the meeting, but *failed* to appear."

FAKE

Both as a noun and as a verb, *fake*, which a decade ago was classed as colloquial, is now in reputable use. Likewise, *bogus*, an Americanism that was originally slang, has won complete acceptance. *See also* BOGUS.

FAULT (verb)

Such a sentence as "One cannot fault his performance" is acceptable to only 52 per cent of the Usage Panel of the American Heritage Dictionary. The dictionary says the use of *fault* as a transitive verb "has been much censured in its more recent vogue." It is difficult to see why this should be so, especially since that use has been in the language since the sixteenth century, though admittedly it has been considered "rare." In the sense of to find a flaw in, the word is not readily replaceable, nor is it unusual to find a noun used as a verb. Why, then, all the fuss? Three other recent dictionaries can't see why, any more than this taboo destroyer can.

FAZE

Four variants coexist: *faze* and *phase* (both pronounced just the way they look), *feeze* (pronounced with either a long "a" or a long "e") and *feaze* (also pronounced both ways). A few dictionaries classify all four as either colloquial, informal or dialectal. Other more recent ones admit the words to good standing. As for pronunciation, the preference here is for faze, because that is what speakers usually say. As for the standing of the word, the opinion here is that it is legitimate, chiefly because it provides a meaning that synonyms don't quite match. The synonym that comes closest is *daunt*, but that has too high-flown a sound for most contexts. You would not find it appropriate to write, "The champ took two heavy smashes on his chin, but they didn't seem to daunt him a bit.'

FEATURE

To say that "the newspaper *featured* an interview with the President" used to get backs up wherever there were backs burdened with maintaining the purity of the language. But, as is so often the case, if a noun used as a verb serves a real need, such as employment of a single word instead of a phrase, the new meaning gains entry into the list of the legitimate.

FEEL

There are some who would restrict the word *feel* to some relationship to the tactile sense or to the emotions, sentiments or sensitivity. They would rule it out as a synonym for *think, believe* or *consider*. In its foggy past, *feel* derives from a root meaning to grope. That should provide a clue to its proper use: it denotes thinking based on some interior awareness. Therefore, the rulers-out should not be allowed to rule out; nevertheless the word should not be used indiscriminately. It may be quite proper to write, "The jury *felt* that the defendant was guilty," but not, "The dean *felt* that students should attend classes punctually."

FEY

Here is another word that brings to arms the members of

the OMIOM academy (Original Meaning Is the Only Meaning). They contend that *fey* properly means doomed to die and that anything else is a perversion of the word. Actually the word has had an unusual progression in which the doomed idea was only one step. It moved from cowardly, hostile, to outlawed and therefore doomed, thence and hence to having a sense of imminent death, then and therefore to otherworldly and thus to visionary, "tetched in the head" or slightly daft. One meaning of the word, of course, remains doomed to die, but words, like men and trees, grow and sometimes change, and *fey* has taken on new, additional aspects over the years.

FIRSTLY

For some reason, there have been grammarians in the past who have objected to *firstly*, though they have never objected to *secondly*, *thirdly* or *seven-hundred sixteenthly*. Even a recent liberal book, Jerome Shostak's *Concise Dictionary of Current American Usage*, says that "*firstly* is at present accepted only on the colloquial level." Oddly enough, the older Webster II is not that restrictive. "Many," it says, "prefer the word *first* in this use"—and lets it go at that. There is no logic to the arbitrary proscription; if *secondly* is acceptable, so should *firstly* be. And it is. However, it should be noted that *first* is as much an adverb as *firstly*. Why not, then, use the simpler sequence *first, second, third,* which incidentally will obviate the need to say *thirty-fourthly?*

FIT, FITTED

No doubt you have seen the entry BET, BETTED, in which Mr. Bierce was spanked for insisting on using the "regular" ("-ed") form for the past tense and participle form of several verbs. If you have, this is a good place to forget it—but for this entry only. Although in ordinary speech it may be acceptable to say, "The role *fit* him like a glove," in careful writing it would have to be *fitted*. The same goes for *befit* and *outfit*.

FIX (noun)

Four nounal uses of *fix* have come into being and they represent different gradations of reputability. In the sense of the ascertained position of an airplane or ship the word is standard. In the sense of a predicament there is some disagreement among dictionaries, but the latest ones rank it either as acceptable or at worst informal. In the sense of a case of bribery or collusion two dictionaries find it standard and one labels it slang. The vote here would go for the ranking of standard (which is inevitable sooner or later in any case) because it is a necessary word for which there is no substitute. In the sense of an injection of heroin the unanimous opinion is that the word is slang.

FIX (verb)

An all-purpose word, the verb *fix* has something like two dozen meanings and though most of them constitute loose or imprecise usage there is no reason to banish them. The Latin root of the word means fasten, and most of the present-day senses are related to the notion of establishing, securing, giving stability, repairing or rendering definition, a notion that is not too remote from that of fasten. However, the line might well be drawn somewhere. A good place to draw it is around the neck of the man who writes, "I'll *fix* you for this" or, still worse, "I'm *fixing* to go to Chicago tomorrow." In general, though many meanings of *fix* may be tolerable, it is often preferable to use a less nebulous, more precise word.

FOLLOWING

Following began life as a participle and some grammarians insist it must stay that way: *"Following* the guide, the hikers trudged through a thick wood." More and more, however, the word has taken on the aspect of a preposition: *"Following* the bomb explosion, three men were arrested." Is this, as some maintain, a dangling participle? Not at all. Many participles have graduated to the "absolute" class or the prepositional class: "Barring accidents, the trip should take an hour," "Speaking of flowers, how do you like this orchid?" (See DANGLING AND NONDANGLING PARTICIPLES in *Syntax Scarecrows.*) *Following* has graduated to this class. The updated Fowler reluctantly concedes the point, but tries to attach a string to it thus: "Its prepositional use . . . can be justified only if it implies something more than a merely temporal connexion between two events, something more than 'after' but less than 'in consequence of.' It can do so in the newspaper report 'Following the disturbances in Trafalgar Square last night, six men will appear at Bow Street this morning.' . . ." This is a fine distinction to make and it is safe to say that writers are not likely to make it. The Fowler text points out that often *following* is merely a formal word for *after,* implying that the simpler word would be preferable. No dissent here.

FOLLOWING, THE

This was another Bierce bugaboo. Here is what he said about the phrase: " 'Washington wrote the following.' The following what? Put in the noun. '*The following* animals are ruminants.' It is not the animals that follow, but their names." The first half of the passage concerns the transformation of an adjective into a noun. It may well be that in Bierce's day the transformation of the adjective *following* into a noun had not yet been accomplished. But it assuredly has been accomplished in our day. Nor is such a conversion unusual; it is a process that has been going on in the language since the earliest times. The word *adjective* itself is an example, as are *general, private, local, express, documentary, spectacular, sedative, prophylactic* and a host of others. As to the second half of the Bierce pronunciamento, it is best dismissed as pure nit-picking.

FRACTION

The point is sometimes made that since ninety-nine one-hundredths is as much a *fraction* as one-tenth, we should not use the word to describe a small part of something. The point is pedantic. Through generations of usage *fraction* has taken on the meaning of a small part. Still, in the interest of precision it is better for the careful writer to say exactly what he means.

FRONT RUNNER

Strictly speaking in the sports sense, a *front runner* is one who does well in a race when he is in the lead (with the implication that he doesn't do so well when he is behind). But in a derived and perhaps more commonly used sense, a *front runner* is simply one who is in the lead in a political or other kind of contest. There is no reason why the term cannot be extended legitimately to take in this secondary sense.

Pinch hitter is another sports term that is occasionally the subject of a caution from the strict speakers. In baseball, where the term was coined, a pinch hitter is a player sent in to bat, not merely as a replacement, but as a batsman that the manager thinks will do better than the man he is replacing. In a derived sense a pinch hitter is anyone hastily substituted for the regular performer and usually not expected to be even as good: an alderman asked to make a speech in place of a Senator who broke his arm reaching into a pork barrel or a stage manager recruited to play the part of the clergyman in place of the actor who showed up drunk. Here, too, there is no objection to the extended meaning, aside from the fact that it is a tired old cliché.

GOT, HAVE

The authorities who write about *have got* agree that it is more common in colloquial, i.e., spoken, language than in literary language. Bierce, however, confuses the issue by citing the example, "I *have got* a good horse," which, he says, "directs attention rather to the act of getting than to the state of having, and represents the capture as recently completed." The trouble here is that in spoken language the statement "I *have got* a good horse" is about as unlikely to be uttered as "Why did I not listen to you?" What a speaker would almost certainly say in the horse example is "I've got a good horse," and that version nullifies Bierce's comment.

Perhaps the revised Fowler is more illuminating on the subject: " 'Have got' for 'possess' has long been good colloquial English, but its claim to be good literary English is not universally conceded. The OED calls it 'familiar,' the COD 'colloquial.' It has, however, the authority of Dr. Johnson (*'He has got a good estate' does not always mean that he has acquired, but barely that he possesses it*), and has long been used by many good writers. Philip Ballard in a spirited defence, citing not only Johnson but also Shakespeare, Swift and Ruskin, concludes, 'The only inference we can draw is that it is not a real error but a counterfeit invented by schoolmasters.' Acceptance of this verdict is here recommended."

Here, too. When an American uses *have got,* or more

commonly the contracted form of *have*, he is referring to
mere possession. When he uses *have gotten*, he is referring
to the act of acquisition. (*See* GOTTEN.) That does not
mean, however, that in written English either form is necessarily desirable; both have a decidedly informal flavor.

GOTTEN

One turn-of-the-century stickler said that *gotten* for *got*
had gone out of good use. Whether it had even in his day is
dubious, but as of today in America it has not. It may not
be the best usage, but it is surely acceptable. In Britain this
is not so. The British still frown on the word and in doing
so have deprived themselves of a linguistic distinction that
is perhaps not indispensable but is sometimes useful. On
both sides of the Atlantic a person would be likely to say,
"The candidate *has got* the votes to win," meaning he has
possession of them. (Admittedly, on either side of the
ocean omission of *got* would lend a slight literary improvement.) But whereas an American might say, "The candidate *has gotten* the votes to win," meaning he has acquired
them, the Briton would feel compelled to substitute *acquired* or *obtained* or *garnered* or *collected* or something
else for *gotten*. Notice that we have been treating here of
spoken English. In written English substitution of the more
precise word is to be preferred.

GRAMMATICAL ERROR

A letter writer tells me: "I have been taught that the expression *grammatical error* is a contradiction in terms. If
something is grammatical, it is correct in so far as the grammar is concerned. Is that right?" No, it is wrong. If a specter
can be a chestnut, this supposed error is one. It appears as
an entry in at least two books on usage, and this one makes
three. The word *grammatical* can mean in conformity with

the rules of grammar, but a much more common meaning is pertaining to grammar and that is the sense in which it is used and understood in the cited phrase. There is no more reason to question this phrase than there is to question the combination *ill health.*

GROOM

In designating a man about to put his head in the marital halter, *groom* is less common in Britain than it is in this country, although the OED dates its use to 1604. In either country it is regarded as unrefined, perhaps because of its association with a manservant who cares for horses. But just as the use of horses in everyday life has dwindled, so the obloquy attaching to *groom* has diminished. Nevertheless, *bridegroom* is still to be preferred in reputable writing.

GROW SMALLER

Trouble-trackers have been known to object to *grow smaller* on the basis that if something grows it gets larger, not smaller. They may be safely ignored, nay, scorned. Just about every dictionary gives as one meaning of *grow* to become.

GUEST

Some newspaper editors have objected to describing persons who patronize hotels or restaurants as *guests,* on the ground that they pay for the hospitality received. There is nothing in the derivation of the word or in the way in which it has been used over the years to support the notion that a *guest* must be nonpaying. The underlying idea of the word is stranger, not freeloader.

HEALTHY, HEALTHFUL

Is it all right to say, "He works in a *healthy* outdoor occupation"? No matter how much the purists kick and scream, the answer would have to be yes. Strictly speaking, *healthy* denotes good physical condition and *healthful* applies to that which is conducive to that condition. But there can be no doubt that *healthy* has taken over both meanings in reputable usage. Anyone who wishes to speak strictly is at liberty to do so, but he is not at liberty to rebuke those who choose to use *healthy* in both senses. A third sense of the word, however, is open to question. The meaning sizable or vigorous, as in "He got a *healthy* kick in the pants," is approved in a couple of dictionaries but has an unmistakable flavor of slang about it.

HECTIC

Despite the resistance of some authorities, such as Fowler and Partridge, *hectic* in the sense of feverish or fully packed and excited is now admitted to the ranks of standard words. In its primary meaning it pertains to a wasting physical condition like tuberculosis, but its association with chronic fever led to its application to feverish conditions and continual excitement, activity, confusion.

HEIGHT, IN

Some obscure editor on some obscure newspaper, speaking out of an obscure mind, once must have told his hired hands not to write, "Jones is 6 feet 2 inches *in height*." His reason remains just as obscure as everything else about him. Perhaps he believed that one does not think of a man in terms of height, as one does a mountain or a building, or perhaps he was merely intent on saving a word by using *tall* instead of *in height*. In any event, his prejudice is largely forgotten these days. The most that can be said is that *tall* is more commonly used.

HELPMATE, HELPMEET

Here we have a comedy of errors. The King James Bible, in Genesis ii, 18, referring to the need for providing a better half for Adam, has the Lord saying, "I will make him an help meet for him." *Help* here meant a person who affords assistance and *meet* meant suitable. Early dictionaries, committing Error No. 1, hyphenated the two words to produce *help-meet*. Later users dropped the hyphen and married the two words. Then came Error No. 2 when some writers apparently thought that *helpmeet* didn't make any sense—which it didn't—and decided the proper word must be *helpmate*. And so today we are stuck with two corrupted words. Of the two, *helpmate* is the more common, though *helpmeet* cannot be tagged archaic, as Partridge classifies it.

HIJACK

Originally slang, the verb *hijack*, together with the nouns *hijacking* and *hijacker*, may now be considered a standard English word or something very close to it. It came into common use in the 1920's during Prohibition, when it meant to steal bootleg liquor or other contraband in transit. When Prohibition was killed, the word remained alive because it conveyed a meaning not provided by any other word. Indeed, it entered upon a broader career: It now denotes the illegal taking over of a land, sea or air conveyance or its contents in transit. Sometimes its meaning is further expanded to include action beyond the takeover, as in "The plane was *hijacked* to Cuba." The word has achieved respectability, even though the deeds it describes have not. It has even had an offspring: The seizure of airplanes has introduced, now and again, the word *skyjack*.

HOLD

For many years I thought I must be suffering from hallucinations when I recalled editors who objected to the use of *hold* in relation to a dinner, a benefit or a meeting. In one moment I was certain an editor had once said that to hold a dinner meant that it was not thrown up, but in the next moment I was equally certain that I must have imagined it because the contention was too absurd. Not long ago, however, Roy H. Copperud reported in his column in Editor & Publisher that he had received a letter from a P.R. man saying: "Some 50 years ago when I began newspapering, I worked for a managing editor who was—happily—a stickler for style. One of his rules was that to *hold* is to grasp. In other words, a meeting is never *held*. Neither is a fair, an election, a dinner, and on and on." So I was not imagining things after all. But I wish I had been. The verb *hold*, which, like *fix* and *get*, is a word of many parts, is completely acceptable in the sense of celebrate, conduct, observe or arrange for, and has been for a good long time.

HOME, HOUSE

Sentimentalists contend that what the builder constructs is a *house* and that the occupants then make it a *home*. But in spite of the sentimentalists that distinction has all but disappeared. Real estate operators selling houses lure prospective buyers with the word *home*, and prospective buyers go along with that designation because they picture themselves as purchasing not structures but abodes. On the other hand, when they get around to selling their structures they are more likely to say, "I am selling my *house*," than to say,

"I am selling my *home.*" In most uses, however, the words are interchangeable.

In the adverbial sense of *at home* the British frown on the word *home.* They do not say, "She is remaining *home* tonight," as Americans often do, but insist on *at home.* Nevertheless, they do not boggle at saying, "She is going *home.*" They do seem inconsistent.

HONEYMOON

Some conservative newspaper society pages rule out the use of *honeymoon* and replace it with *wedding trip,* apparently on the basis of Bierce's objection to the word. "Moon here means month," said he, "so it is incorrect to say, 'a week's honeymoon,' or, 'Their honeymoon lasted a year.'" *Moon* does bear a relationship to *month,* but the etymological evidence suggests that *honeymoon* originally referred not to that period but rather to the waxing and waning of the affection of the newlyweds like the waxing and waning of the moon. Be that as it may, there is no reason to be as literal-minded about the word as Bierce was. For centuries it has referred to the holiday spent just after marriage, regardless of the time period. Literal-mindedness of that kind would forbid the common figurative extension of the word to mean a new period of harmony, as in "the President's *honeymoon* with Congress." Heaven forfend. Presidents have enough trouble with Congress without denying them a *honeymoon.*

HOPEFULLY

On the door of her home in The Springs on Long Island, N.Y., Jean Stafford, Pulitzer Prize writer, has the following notice posted: "The word HOPEFULLY must not be misused on these premises. Violators will be humiliated." One can sympathize with Miss Stafford's attitude. In its logical and primary meaning *hopefully* denotes in a hopeful manner. And yet . . . And yet . . . More and more the word is being used—and no doubt overused—to mean it is to be hoped. The reason is evident: No other word in English expresses that thought. In a single word we can say it is regrettable that (*regrettably*) or it is fortunate that (*fortunately*) or it is lucky that (*luckily*), and it would be comforting if there were such a word as *hopably* or, as suggested by Follett, *hopingly*, but there isn't. And so writers produce such sentences as, "Negotiations have now begun, hopefully with peace as the outcome." The question then arises whether the arbiters of usage would not be well advised to yield. In this instance nothing is to be lost—the word would not be destroyed in its primary meaning—and a useful, nay necessary, term is to be gained. There are plenty of precedents in English for the acceptance of "distorted" meanings of words: *internecine, fruition, alibi, nice* and *shambles*, to cite a few. The newer dictionaries are beginning to open their arms to the "incorrect" meaning of *hopefully* (with the strange exception of the permissive Webster III, which ducks the issue altogether). The American Heritage says in its first edition that the new meaning is acceptable to "only 44 per cent" of its usage panel, but there are indications that that figure will rise in the next edition. Webster's New World in its Second College Edition says of the latter-day meaning, "regarded by some as loose usage, but widely current." And the Random House accepts it without question. The word is in common use and perhaps in reputable use and one wonders whether attempts to resist it are not exercises in futility. It would be well to keep in mind Louis Kronenberger's perceptive passage about published guides to usage: "Handbooks clearly have their place, and when they

put their finger in the dike rather than bid the waves stand
still, have a very real value as well." * Note especially the
phrase about bidding the waves stand still. (P.S. At the moment of going to press Miss Stafford made it clear she was
not giving in.)

HUMAN

The OED labels *human* used as a noun as "Now chiefly
humorous or affected." Partridge, writing a couple of decades later, says: "As a noun, *human* is either a jocularity, or
an affectation; it may, however, make its way as a conven-
ience." Hmm, the authorities seem to be giving ground.
Webster II and all recent dictionaries accept the noun completely. The authorities have indeed given ground. And
there is every reason why they should. The conversion of
adjectives into nouns is an ancient process in the English
language. There is no more cause for rejecting the noun
human than there is for rejecting the noun *anthropoid*.

IDENTIC, IDENTICAL

Identic, as all agree, is not in use outside the world of
diplomacy, and even there the present-day tendency is to
replace it with *identical*. Most authorities insist that *identic*
implies exactly the same wording if a diplomatic note is
being spoken of, or exactly the same form if an action is
involved. Of course, even in an *identic* note there will be
variations in "trim"—the names of the addressees, the salu-
tations, the pronominal references, the signatories—but
everything else will be precisely the same. The revised
Fowler, however, says that *identic* means "the same in sub-
stance rather than completely identical in wording." That
is not the view in diplomatic circles, but the difference is
admittedly minuscule.

* "American Lingo," *The Atlantic*, September 1970.

IF, WHETHER

At one time grammarians maintained that the conjunction *if* had to be restricted to introducing clauses of condition or supposition; it could not be used as a synonym for *whether*, they said. If this was ever true, it surely has not been true in modern times. Doubt is expressed here about its ever having been true because we find in the King James version of Genesis viii, 8, "Also he sent forth a dove from him, to see if the waters were abated from off the face of the ground." The dove, says the Bible, "found no rest for the sole of her foot." Those old-time grammarians are in the same situation; maybe in the same boat.

There is one situation, however, in which *whether* is definitely to be preferred. When the noun clause begins the sentence, *if* might be momentarily confusing because it could suggest a condition: "If he planned to run for reelection was the information sought by the questioners."

See also WHETHER OR NOT *under Syntax Scarecrows.*

ILL HEALTH   *See* GRAMMATICAL ERROR.

INCOMPARABLES

How can one line be straighter than another? If a line is straight, then by golly it's straight, and if it isn't straight then it isn't straight, and that's that. That's what? That's the way some nigglers attempt to handcuff us in our use of language. They contend that many words are absolutes that do not admit of comparison. Partridge, for example, has drawn up a list of about eighty such words, with the implication that there are quite a few more. He includes *certain* (but I am less certain about that one than he is); he includes *complete* in a list that is more complete than any compiled elsewhere; he includes *obvious* and that is almost the most obvious misfit of them all.

If one wishes to niggle, almost any adjective can be regarded as an absolute. But common sense tells us to avoid any such binding position. The proper course is to respect the absoluteness of words that become ridiculous if comparative or superlative degrees are attached to them (Orwell's *more equal*, for instance) or of words that should be preserved in their pristine meanings because they are irreplaceable (*unique*, for instance). A list of such words could be quite short: *equal, eternal, fatal, final, infinite, perfect* (despite the Constitution's "more perfect union"), *supreme, total, unanimous, unique* and probably *absolute* itself, though it is conceivable that one dictator's rule could be more absolute than another's.

INSANE ASYLUM

Says Bierce: "Obviously an asylum cannot be unsound in mind. Say asylum for the insane." Shall we, then, also banish *foreign correspondent, madhouse* (dating to 1687), *dramatic critic, juvenile court, criminal lawyer, psychiatric clinic* and *civil engineer?* To pose the question is to expose the ridiculousness of the objection. Adjectives are not always confined to a single narrow meaning. Many of them have coordinate meanings, such as characterized by, used by, designed for, derived from. It is one of the conveniences of English, and especially American English, that thoughts can be compressed into a couple of words instead of requiring elaborate phrases; thus, *insane asylum* rather than *asylum for the insane*. Of course, *insane asylum* is avoided these days for a quite different reason: It is too harsh, it does not meet the euphemistic requirements of the day. And so we are more likely to say *mental hospital* or *home for the mentally disturbed*.

INSIGNIA

Time was when *insignia* was exclusively a plural, the singular being *insigne*. But no more; the old Latin singular has just about vanished. *Insignia* is now regarded as a singular noun and has even given birth to a plural of its own—*insignias*—in the same way as has *agenda*. *Insignia* can still be used as a plural, but usually isn't.

INTERNECINE

There is a sufficiency of words meaning deadly or bloody or characterized by slaughter, which is what *internecine* in its original sense means, since it derives from the Latin root *necare* (to kill). But in its later sense of mutually destructive or pertaining to conflict among members of the same group it is just about irreplaceable. Hence, in this sense it not only is completely established but also has taken precedence over the original meaning.

INTERPRETATIVE, INTERPRETIVE

Both forms are acceptable. Probably because of disapproval of *preventative* in favor of *preventive* some of the blackening has brushed off on *interpretative*. Webster II characterizes *preventative* as an "irregularly formed doublet," but that does not apply to *interpretative*.

KILLED INSTANTLY

The superstition taken up here is not at all a common one but it perhaps illustrates the kind of thinking that gives rise to such things. A newspaper publisher once questioned the sentence, "The driver of the car was killed instantly in the crash." "Killed instantly?" he said. "How else can you be killed?" Well, for one thing you can be killed by inches (the phrase appears in Webster II) as, for instance, by torture. Or, for another thing, people can be killed by famine, a process that might take a year or more. Some will argue that death, at any rate, is instantaneous, that one instant a person is alive and the next he is dead. But even that point is not completely resolved, as the debates surrounding heart transplants have demonstrated: Is a patient dead when the heart stops beating or when the electric impulses in the brain drop off or when?

So much, then, for *killed instantly* and that much should also take care of any similar objection to *sudden death*. The next question that will be raised is entirely foreseeable. Someone is going to ask, "Instead of *instantly*, don't you mean *instantaneously?*" Ho hum.

LAST, PAST, LATEST

Over the decades the pedants have attempted to pose two problems. One involves *last* versus *past* and the other involves *last* versus *latest*. They will be taken up in that order.

Long asserted that you should prefer "last two weeks, last six months &c., to past two weeks, past six months, &c." Bierce disagreed. He said: "Neither is accurate: a week cannot be the last if another is already begun; and all weeks except this one are past. Here two wrongs seem to make a right: we can say the week last past. But will we? I trow not." You know where he can trow that, don't you? If ever an argument set up a straw man, that one does. Since the days of Middle English the words *last* and *past* have been used interchangeably to mean gone by immediately before the present. They still may be so used.

As to *last* versus *latest*, Long again had an opinion: "*Last* is used of place or order; *latest* of time." Here, too, an attempt is made to draw a distinction that, however much it may appeal to logic, ignores usage and the history of the language. Since the days of Middle English *last* has been used to mean most recent. As we are told by Follett—and no permissivist he—the distinction between the two words "has virtually disappeared." If it ever existed.

LENGTHY

There are those who disparage this word; one critic says it is "no better than breadthy or thicknessy." That may well be. Still the word has been in the language for almost three centuries and rash would be he who tried to get rid of it at this late date. True enough, it says more than *long*; it connotes overlong or tedious or prolix. The mere mention of those equivalents shows how unnecessary *lengthy* is. But if a writer wishes to use it, let us not gainsay him.

LIT

Despite objections that are heard from time to time, *lit* is usually just as acceptable as *lighted*. Evans in *CW* says this has always been true. "*Lighted* seems much commoner," he adds, "when the past participle is used as an adjective. It would seem more 'natural' to most Americans to refer to 'a lighted match' rather than to 'a lit match.'" That is right, but, if he will hold that match for a moment, in the simple past tense it seems more natural to say "He lit the match" than to say "He lighted the match."

LOAN

Although most expert users of English dislike *loan* as a verb ("I *loaned* him my pen"), except in financial contexts, it must be acknowledged that the usage is sanctioned by dictionaries. If you are not offended by "Friends, Romans, countrymen, *loan* me your ears" or by "Distance *loans* enchantment," you may go along with the dictionaries and you will always have a defense.

-LY   *See* ADVERBS.

MAD

If *mad* is not completely acceptable in the sense of angry, it is the doing of some of our teachers. Evans points
his finger right at them when he says that the word's "familiar sense, 'moved by anger,' has been in use so long and
so universally that it would unquestionably be accepted as
standard had not purist teachers made it the special target
of their disapprobation." As Evans indicates, the "angry"
meaning is not a recent development. In the Bible, the
102d Psalm says, "They that are *mad* against me, are
sworne against me," and Acts xxvi, II, offers, "And being
exceedingly *mad* against them, I persecuted them even
unto strange cities." Shakespeare, in *The Merchant of Ven-
ice*, writes, "Now, in faith, Gratiano, you give your wife too
unkind a cause of grief; an 'twere to me, I would be *mad* at
it." Back in 1882 Ayres disputed an Englishman who
thought that the Americans, by using *mad* to mean angry,
had "manifestly impaired the language." The impairment,
if any, is certainly not manifest. In any event, unscientific
observation indicates not only that the angry sense of *mad*
is in widespread use but also that it is more common than
the insane sense, among both educated and uneducated
speakers and writers. The prohibition of the purists is not
likely to last long.

MAP A PLAN

An uncle of mine who was a civil engineer* by profession
and a nit-picker by obsession used to object to the locution
"map a plan," which appears occasionally in newspaper
headlines. He found it a redundancy, since essentially a
plan is a map. He had half a point, but the exigencies of

* Speaking of *civil engineer*, see INSANE ASYLUM.

headline writing being what they are, the locution cannot be condemned very strongly.

This same uncle also disliked the expression "make a motion," used in the parliamentary sense. He would say that a Senator doesn't make a motion; he moves. It seems reasonable to suppose that underneath the nit-picker's engineering façade he was really a copy editor and couldn't tolerate the use of three words where one would do.

MIDAIR

The objection, it must be confessed, was an isolated one, yet an editor did question the word *midair*. "Why say 'The planes crashed in *midair*'?" he asked. "What's the matter with plain *air*?" He went on to ask where *midair* was. The answer according to Webster II is "neither very close to nor very far from the ground." There! That should enlighten the editor. To be sure, the word is not very specific nor very informative. Yet it is in good use. So let's ignore the editor.

MOMENTARILY, MOMENTLY

Perhaps it would have been well to cling to the distinction whereby *momentarily* means for only a short time ("He lost his footing *momentarily*") and *momently* means at any moment ("He will arrive *momently*"). Unfortunately, however, the use of *momently* is becoming rarer and rarer as the years go by. *Momentarily* is now reputably used in both senses and there is no use in fighting it.

MOTORCADE   *See* CAVALCADE.

NAKED, NUDE

Perhaps the distinction is subjective, but *naked* seems to be, shall we say, the barer word. Indeed, *nude* in the sense of unclothed did not come into common use until the mid-nineteenth century, which suggests it was a euphemism for *naked*. Nowadays, except in the specialized use in the art field ("Michelangelo enjoyed painting *nudes*"), the words are just about interchangeable.

NEARLY, ALMOST

Long attempted to draw a distinction between these two words on the basis that *nearly* applies to quantity, time or space, whereas *almost* generally applies to degree. Well, maybe. Frederick T. Wood in *Current English Usage* suggests that *almost* is "what we might call a 'minus' word; it subtracts from the idea of the word it modifies. *Nearly*, on the other hand, represents an approach towards it, and therefore gives it more emphasis." Again, maybe. Usually the distinction between the two words is so subtle that a speaker would have to retreat to the next room and cogitate before deciding which to use. The answer is that normally the distinction is not worth the trouble. Wood does make one useful point, however: In denoting feeling or state of mind *almost* is used. Thus you would not use *nearly* in such sentences as, "I am *almost* afraid to make the trip," and "He *almost* wished he had never met her."

NECESSARIES, NECESSITIES

After pointing out that *necessaries* means essentials or requisites, Partridge goes on to say that "in this sense, *necessities* is obsolete—or, at the least, obsolescent." The truth is almost the reverse so far as American usage is concerned. *Necessities*, the stronger word of the two, is crowding out *necessaries* in the United States. One reason may be, as Evans suggests, that until fairly recently *necessary* was a euphemism in some rural areas for a privy or a chamber pot.

NORMALCY

It probably wasn't Warren Harding but his speech-writer who unfurled the word *normalcy* in 1920 in a Harding speech that provoked derision among the intelligentsia. But it wasn't Harding (or his speech-writer) who coined the word; according to the OED it dates back at least to 1857. It thus has some credentials of a standard word. But whether it is a needful variant of the more common *normality* is another question.

NOSTALGIA

Here again is a word that has departed from its original meaning but that in most quarters has been cheered on its way. It derives from Greek words meaning "return home" and "pain" and thus, in its original sense, means an almost painful yearning for home—acute homesickness. But writers searching for a word meaning a pleasant-painful or perhaps poignant longing for a past time or for something recalled from a former time found no word that conveyed that thought. They turned to *nostalgia*, which did seem to communicate the idea, and it is now well-established in the derived meaning. Nor is there any loss to the language: The writer who wishes to speak of homesickness can always write *homesickness*, and qualify it with an adjective if that seems necessary.

NOUNS AS ADJECTIVES

Objections have been raised to the use of nouns as adjectives, but set forth in that fashion the objections are misguided. Objections can be validly raised only against the overuse of nouns as adjectives. Any noun in English may be employed adjectivally and there can be no doubt that such alterations of function have enriched the language and made it more flexible. There can be no questioning of *population explosion* or *storm warnings* or *stock market*. There could be objection, however, to *atom arms proliferation ban* or *trade report leak inquiry*. With the introduction of those phrases one cat has crept out of the bag: Newspaper headlines have exerted a large and sometimes deplorable influence on the language. But it should be said by way of extenuation that the headline writer is forced into his noun-adjective pile-up by the inflexible space restrictions he faces. A comparable extenuation may be granted to today's scientists, astronauts and technicians, who are compelled by the complexity of their endeavors to resort to the kind of shorthand that gives us, for example, *descent orbit insertion burn*. But the extension of this practice to other fields in which it is scarcely necessary is more difficult to excuse. Manufacturers and their advertising minions take it up in the hope that some of the aura of science and technology will rub off on their products. Thus you may find that your television set contains something called a *perma-set tuning control* or that your motorcar is equipped with *6-plunger fuel injection and 7-main-bearing crankshaft*. This is the sort of thing that has gone too far, not the mere use of nouns as adjectives.

NOUNS AS VERBS

Just as nouns may be made into adjectives (*see* NOUNS AS ADJECTIVES), so they may be converted into verbs. Such conversions have been going on since the thirteenth century, and the language has been the better for them. Objection can be raised to transformations of this kind only if they are introduced solely for the sake of novelty and result in totally unnecessary words. It is unobjectionable to take the noun *garden* and convert it into a verb so that one can say, "When he is in the country he reads and *gardens*," instead of having to say, "reads and cultivates a plot of ground." That is an example of a useful word. On the other hand, it is sheer affectation and novelty-hunting to say, "The novelist has a house in the country where he *authors* his books." *Authors* says nothing that the common word *writes* does not say; it is as superfluous and tasteless as monogrammed toilet tissue. Let us not, then, arbitrarily rule out all noun-to-verb conversions (*see* CONTACT, *for example*), but let us not burden the language with needless novelties.

NTH DEGREE

Fowler, writing from a literal mathematical point of view, finds *to the nth degree* "wrong" when used to mean to the utmost or to an extreme. Mathematically speaking, it is wrong because it connotes lacking specification, indefinite. However, in nonmathematical common usage it is generally sanctioned, though it bears the faint aroma of a cliché. Even the conservative Webster II accepted it years and years ago.

NUBILE

From a Latin root meaning to marry, *nubile* in its primary meaning denotes a suitability by age or condition for marriage; it usually applies to females. But many words grow from their roots, just as a tree does. If they did not, a *homely* girl would be one who merely stayed at home, and many a homely girl wishes it were so. Just as *homely* has expanded to mean more than that, so in recent years *nubile* has expanded to mean sexually attractive. A place can be found for that meaning, unless you prefer *sexy*, which is a casual word that many dictionaries frown upon.

NUMEROUS

Here we have another of the many oddities of Bierce. His entry under this word says: "Numerous for Many. Rightly used, *numerous* relates to numbers, but does not imply a great number. A correct use is seen in the term numerous verse—verse consisting of poetic numbers; that is, rhythmical feet." He could hardly have been more wrong or more perverse. *Numerous* to mean many was in good use as far back as 1622, according to the OED. On the other hand, his "correct" use has for some time been labeled either archaic or rare.

ONTO

For some mysterious reason Cowles characterizes *onto* as colloquial and implies it is not to be used in reputable writing. The facts are (a) that it has been in the language since 1581; (b) that it bears the same relation to *on* that *into*, assuredly a respectable word, bears to *in*; and (c) that it is a necessary word because it often means something different from *on*. Item (c) is readily demonstrated when you consider that a person walking *onto* the terrace is not doing the same thing as a person walking *on* the terrace.

ORATE

Some books on usage condemn *orate* as either facetious or a humorous barbarism. The word is, to be sure, a back formation from *oration*, but that fact in itself is not enough to condemn it; *diagnose, scavenge, donate* and *drowse* are also back formations and their credentials are not questioned these days. The worst that can be said about *orate* is that it has a disparaging connotation: It implies pomposity or pretentiousness. (*See* BACK FORMATIONS.)

OTHERWISE

Fowler worked himself into a thousand-word lather over what he deemed misuses of *otherwise*. Starting from the premise that the word was an adverb ("He decided, sensibly or *otherwise*, to take a chance"), he denounced its extension to adjectival use ("No further threats, economic or *otherwise*, have been made") and to nounal use ("The electorate may be consulted on the merits, or *otherwise*, of a single specific measure"). One may borrow a bit of the Fowler lather to shave off into discredited oblivion the nounal uses—first, because they do sound unnatural, and second, because they are usually readily replaced: e.g., "the merits or demerits." As to the adjectival uses, they have become so common and accepted that the "correct" form, using *other* rather than *otherwise* ("No further threats, economic or *other*"), has an almost pedantic sound to modern ears. It may be added that, according to the OED, the adjectival use was standard as far back as 1400.

OVER

Some copy editors in all parts of this country and perhaps in other parts of the English-speaking world consistently change "*over* $150" to "*more than* $150." The origin of this bit of superstitious tinkering is not clear, but it may be friend Bierce again. He objected to *over* in this sense and found *upward of* equally objectionable. He gave no reason for the objection and it is difficult to see how there could be any. Since the days of late Middle English the meaning *in excess of* has been in reputable use. Strangely enough, those who dislike *over* do not hesitate to write "*above* $150." Nor do they boggle at *just over*, probably because *just more than* won't do. The only objectionable use of *over* is an instance in which it is used illogically: "Profits declined 13 per cent *over* the previous year." Here the word would have to be *from*.

As to *upward of* (which is preferred in the United States to *upwards of*), the perfectly valid phrase means *more than*. But, unbelievable as it may seem, the OED says that since

1613 the phrase has also meant *rather less than*. In some parts of the United States that meaning, together with the meaning *approximately*, is extant, but Webster II properly labels it "erron. & dial."

PARTIALLY, PARTLY

The word *partially* has two meanings: (1) with bias or partiality; (2) in part. Both meanings have been in standard use for centuries. Nevertheless, among some editors the word is taboo in its second meaning. Those editors are right if, and only if, there is some chance of ambiguity. That kind of chance might arise in a sentence such as, "The judge ruled *partially* for the defendant." It would not arise in a sentence such as, "The sun was *partially* eclipsed." It must be acknowledged, however, that the simpler word *partly* would serve at least as well in either instance.

PASS A RESOLUTION

A few journalistic comma-chasers forbid the use of *pass* to denote the approval of a resolution by a deliberative body and insist on *adopt*. The reasoning, if any, behind this is not apparent. It may have something to do with the kind of resolution the individual shapes in his mind; for example, he *adopts* a resolution on New Year's Eve not to beat his wife any more. But obviously an individual could not *pass* such a resolution in any event. A deliberative body, however, can and does *pass* resolutions. Indeed, the illustrative quotation that appears in the OUD reads: "The *passing* by the House of Commons of such a resolution as this."

PAST MASTER

It used to be *passed master*, which, in truth, makes more sense because that version would seem to denote someone who has passed his tests to become a master. *Past master* would seem to mean a former master (and does, indeed, mean that, as well as one who is an expert). However, in referring to the expert it is best to put aside logic and accept the version that has now passed muster: *past master*.

PEOPLE, PERSONS

Around the turn of the century, grammarians adjured writers not to use *people* for persons individually. Since then usage has changed a little so that *people* has gained greater latitude. The emphasis should still be on the connotation of individuality, however. If you write, "Fifty *people* were present," you are thinking of the group, but if you write, "Forty-nine *persons* were injured," you are thinking not of the group but of forty-nine individuals. A general rule might be: Use *people* for large groups presented in round numbers, use *persons* for an exact or small number. In spoken language the latitude for the use of *people* is perhaps somewhat wider. We might well say, "Thirteen *people* were present," whereas we might more properly write, "Thirteen *persons* were present."

PER

Late in the last century Cobbett declared that "10 shillings a bushel" was far preferable to "*per* bushel" because "the *per* is not English, and is, to the greater part of the people, a mystical sort of word." Later on Long wrote in the same vein, "Do not use *per* before English nouns: use *a*." And so newspapermen, following these injunctions, occasionally write, "In Belgium the yield *a* cow *a* year is 3,760 kilograms of milk," or, "The delay in getting to the convention floor was running 25 to 30 minutes *a* newsman." The word *per* is no longer a mystical sort of word and these days is quite appropriate in statistical or economic contexts—in short, in any context, such as the sentences just cited, in which *a* is ludicrous.

PINCH HITTER   *See* FRONT RUNNER.

POISON GAS
It was during one of those big wars, it matters not which, that some editors decided that it was improper to speak of *poison gas* and that the only proper form was *poisonous gas*. But it is another of those instances in which a noun is legitimately used adjectivally. (*See* NOUNS AS ADJECTIVES.)

PORTION
"This word is often incorrectly used for *part*," said Ayres. "A *portion* is properly a part assigned, allotted, set aside for a special purpose; a share, a division." That pronunciamento was issued in 1882 and to this day there are editors and writers who subscribe to it. Ayres's definition of the word was correct as far as it went. The only trouble is that since the days of Middle English the word has also meant simply a part. Thus it is not incorrect to use it in that sense, but the meaning of a share should also be kept in mind.

PRACTICALLY, VIRTUALLY
By strict definition *practically* means, or should mean, in practice or for practical purposes, whereas *virtually* denotes as good as, in effect or almost. By common usage, however, *practically* has practically come to mean virtually the same thing as *virtually*. All authorities do not sanction this overlapping, but they are waging a losing battle, chiefly because attempting to distinguish the meanings usually requires close study of the context. There can be agreement, however, on ruling out the use of *practically* in the sense of "al-

most" where it is obviously out of place: For example, in speaking of a student who completed the required work for a Ph.D. but failed in his final examination you would not say, "He *practically* got the degree."

PRESIDENTIAL AND SCIENTIST

What's the connection? To the modern mind, none. To some minds of 1896, a very definite one: Both words are incorrect. In particular, to the mind of J. H. Long, M.A., LL.B., who wrote *Slips of Tongue and Pen*, the words are as good (or as bad) as nonexistent. About *presidential* he wrote: "The adjective—if formed at all—ought to be *presidental*. *Presidential campaign* is a very inelegant and ill-constructed expression." About *scientist* he wrote: "Use *scientific man*, savant, &c. If a noun with this meaning is to be formed from *science*, it ought to be *sciencist*, not *scientist*." Today we are not even aware that the two words are malformations. Nor are they rarities; there is ample precedent for the complete acceptance of malformed words. All of which proves, perhaps, that what "ought to be" is not always what "is," and that if one is too doggedly dogmatic, unorthodoxies may grow up to hound one's dogmatism.

PROPOSE, PURPOSE

It is not proper, said one critic in the early 1900's, to say, "I *propose* to go to Europe," because a mere intention is not a proposal. Apparently this was one of the delusions of the day (which in some quarters has persisted to the present) because Ayres, addressing himself to the same distinction, said, "*Propose*, correctly used, means to put forward or to offer for *the consideration of others*." How this notion arose is difficult to determine. As far back as 1500, according to the OUD, *propose* had in addition to that idea, the meaning of "to put before one's own mind as something that one is going to do; to design, purpose, intend." Oddly, however, Partridge, citing the Oxford dictionary, says that "*propose* is encroaching far too freely on the territory of *purpose*." The fact is that the "encroachment" has gone so far that *purpose* as a verb has almost become a rarity.

PROVED, PROVEN

Although *proved*, as the participle, is the preferred form in written English, *proven* is widely used in the spoken language and cannot be set down as incorrect or improper. Even in the written, more formal language, *proven* is frequently used as the participial adjective preceding a noun, as in "a *proven* oil field" or "a *proven* fact."

PROVIDED, PROVIDING

For generations teachers have insisted that the subordinating conjunction is *provided*, not *providing*. No doubt the reasoning behind this distinction was that *provided* is an elliptical form of "it being provided," whereas nothing similar can be said about *providing*. However, nothing similar can be said about *supposing* either, and that word has won acceptance as a conjunction. Because of their early training, many of the pupils of those teachers are conditioned to rejecting *providing*, but the rejection is baseless. The only caution to be sounded about either word is that it should not be used as a straight synonym for *if*; both *provided* and *providing* imply a stipulation of some kind, which *if* does not always imply. For instance, you would not say, "He would not have been injured *provided* he had taken more care," but you could very well say, "He will not be injured, *provided* (or *providing*) he takes all the prescribed precautions."

QUITE

Strictly speaking, *quite* means completely ("He was *quite* wrong") or emphatically, positively ("It is *quite* the thing to do"). Not quite so strictly speaking, *quite* is used to mean rather or somewhat ("It is *quite* foggy in London") and *quite a* is used to mean a substantial but indefinite quantity ("*Quite a* number of dissenters were present"). These secondary, unstrictly speaking meanings may not yet be standard, but they show every sign of thriving and becoming acceptable.

QUOTATION

Under the word *quotation* Follett devotes a fat paragraph to declaring that "it is worth recalling to the exact-minded that speakers make statements, not *quotations*— unless they repeat other speakers' statements. Thus the *New York Times* feature 'Quotation of the Day' should properly read: 'Statement of the Day.' The words become a quotation only when the newspaper reader repeats them to his fellow commuter. If it is argued that the *Times* is quoting the notable words, then every article in the paper is a mosaic of quotations from known and unknown authors, which is absurd. A newspaper reports statements that its readers may turn into quotations, spoken or written." The point being made here does not even qualify as pedantic. What this quodlibet simmers down to is the question, At what remove does the repeater of words have to be from the originator for the words to qualify as a quotation? Follett says at second remove. But why? Deponent saith not. Of course "speakers make statements, not quotations," but as soon as those statements are relayed, whether for the first time or the thousandth time, they are quotations. When the reporter relays them to the reader, they are quotations, enclosed in quotation marks. Let the "exact-minded" consult the basic meaning of the verb *quote*. One definition, in the OUD, is: "To copy out or repeat (a passage, statement, etc.) from a book, document, speech, etc., with some indication that one is giving the words of another 1680." No indication there that the passage has to be repeated to a fellow commuter.

RAISE (noun)

Some newspaper editors used to maintain that workers did not get a *raise*; they got a *pay rise* or an *increase in pay*. (Clearly they were not referring to newspapermen, who in those days got neither.) The point seems to have been that except for a few dialectal or technical uses *raise* was not a noun. For a good many years now, however, *raise* has legitimately meant an increase in remuneration.

RAISE (verb)

In a bygone day it was not uncommon for some authorities to insist that you do not *raise* children; you *bring them up*. Others said you could *bring them up* all right, but still better, you *rear* them. Well, today hardly anyone *rears* children, except pedants over sixty—and what are they doing having children anyway? Plenty of people bring them up, but probably the majority *raise* them. Perhaps a qualification is necessary here: Both Fowler and Partridge indicate that in Britain children are not *raised*, but *reared*, the suggestion being that *raise* in this sense is an Americanism.

RAREBIT

This is one of those odd instances in which the wrong word has been nudging out the right word and nothing can (or should) be done about it. The dish of melted cheese and beer or ale poured over toast was originally and euphemistically and jokingly called *Welsh rabbit* just as codfish was called *Cape Cod turkey*, or sheep testicles were called *mountain oysters* or the hangover remedy of a raw egg with Worcestershire sauce, etc., was called a *prairie oyster*. But someone didn't get the joke and apparently thought *rabbit* was a slurring pronunciation of *rarebit* and the damage was done. Today most menus, if not cookbooks, list *rarebit*.

REDHEAD

Here is a puzzler. The Newswire Stylebook, issued jointly by The Associated Press and The United Press International a few years ago, turned thumbs down on *redhead* (and *redheaded*) for no discernible reason. Roy H. Copperud, writing in *Editor & Publisher*, said: "Although I have searched assiduously, nowhere else have I been able to find any question raised about *redhead* and *redheaded*. The terms have been standard at least since the turn of the century, as indicated by the Century Dictionary." Much longer than that. According to the OED, they date back to Middle English.

REFER BACK

Taking the redundant remand back as an analogy, some nit-pickers have questioned *refer back*, as in, "The bill was *referred back* to committee." The word *back* may in some instances be superfluous, but it is not normally redundant, as it is in *remand back*, *reply back* or *return back*. The notion of *back* is not at all prominent or even necessarily present in the word *refer*, which has as its primary meaning to direct attention to.

RELATION, RELATIVE

Under the foregoing heading, Partridge has only this to say: "The writer is one of those who prefer *relative* to *relation* in the sense 'kinsman.' " To which this book can only say, "Ditto." On the face of it there is something strange here. Many people have the same preference, but dictionaries regard the words as interchangeable. We may keep our preference for *relative*, then, but we can advance no reason for it and surely we cannot foist it on others.

ROB

In legal parlance the word *rob* implies the use of force, and on that basis some trouble-trackers contend that a person cannot *rob* a bank or a church or a store. In nonlegal parlance, however, it is quite possible to *rob* all three. In addition to the legal definition, Webster II says the word means "to strip or deprive by stealing; to plunder; to steal from," and then quotes as an example a line from Shakespeare: "To be executed for *robbing* a church." And, of course, one can *rob* a man of his good name. It would be interesting to ask the trouble-trackers what verb they would use to replace *rob* in describing the act of illegally taking something from a bank, a church or a store. What should be borne in mind, however, is that one cannot *rob* money or jewelry, and it will be borne in mind if you think of *rob* as meaning Relieve Of Booty.

Burglary does demand adherence to legal parlance; it is a particular kind of nonlegal-parlance robbery, involving breaking and entering. *See* BURGLARIZE.

ROOFTOP

Despite the fact that it is an utterly meaningless word when you stop to examine it, *rooftop* now has crept into two dictionaries: Webster III and the Random House. This can only mean that enough people have been going around shouting it from housetops to give it some appearance of legitimacy. For some people and some dictionary-makers that is enough.

'ROUND

Forget the apostrophe. In addition to being a legitimate adjective and noun, *round* is a legitimate preposition and adverb. Therefore save space and ink and write, "the year *round*" and "we showed the visitors *round*." Needless to say, "around" is perfectly good, too.

SABOTAGE

Sir Alan Herbert objected to employing *sabotage* as a verb, "for the robust verb *to wreck* will always do the same work better." Sir Ernest Gowers (in *The Complete Plain Words*) disagreed. He said that words such as *wreck, destroy* or *damage* have not the same implication of disloyalty as *sabotage* has. Up to a point Sir Ernest was right, but he did not go far enough in defining the word. Disloyalty is not always the distinguishing element in sabotage. It is not, for instance, when enemy agents wreck a factory. It is the underhandedness of the wrecking or undermining operation that separates the saboteurs from the ordinary wreckers. The saboteurs may indeed be disloyal, as when disaffected workers damage machinery in a factory, or they may not be, as when a nation's negotiators obstruct an international conference. In any event, Herbert's cause has become a lost one, because the verb *sabotage* is recognized in all dictionaries.

SCAN

In its older and primary meaning, *scan* denotes almost the opposite of its later and more prevalent sense. The older meaning is to scrutinize, to examine closely. The more common and now accepted meaning, which the old OED hasn't heard of and Webster II labels colloq., is to view hastily, to examine superficially.

SCORE

Sometimes the pedants trap themselves in their own pedantry. Bierce, for example, repudiated the use of *score* in such a sentence as, "He scored an advantage over his opponent," arguing that "to *score* is not to win a point, but to record it." It is true that an early meaning of *score* is to make a record. But if we are going to look backward, why stop there? By its derivation from the Old Norse, the word refers to notching. Why not confine it to that meaning? The answer, of course, is that words acquire additional meanings that in time become standard. The point-winning sense of *score* is more than a century old.

SECURE

Objection is validly raised to the use of *secure* as a straight synonym for *obtain* or *get*. But that does not mean that something that is obtained is never *secured*. The connotation of secure is obtaining with certainty. Thus if it had been uncertain whether there were any seats remaining on Flight 812 to Goosepimple, Iowa, the proud travel agent might well and acceptably say, "I secured two seats for you on the plane," even if he didn't quite know how right he was.

SEE

"The second half *saw* Princeton come back with a three-touchdown rally." Stanley Woodward, who was the sports overseer on the old *New York Herald Tribune*, once told the underling who wrote that, "If you ever use *see* again in connection with an inanimate object, I'll fan your tail." The underling never forgot and never had his tail fanned. But he need not have been so timid so far as correctness is concerned. For a century or more *see* has been acceptable in the sense of to be marked by; the OED gives the example,

"Eighteen rivers have *seen* their navigation improved." Mr. Woodward's point should have been that journalists tend to overuse the word in that sense, but when he dragged in the inanimate object notion he had no point at all.

SICK, ILL

If there are any Englishmen around suffering from flu, they will probably shrink from using *sick* to describe their condition. As Fowler explains it, English dislike of the blunt word *vomit* has made them substitute sick for it as a euphemism, leaving them with the word *ill* to denote the generalized sense of an ailing condition. Americans seem to have stronger stomachs; they may not say they feel like vomiting, but they would not hesitate to say that they feel *nauseated* (or more likely *nauseous*, one fears) or even that they feel like *throwing up* or *upchucking*. Then they have no difficulty in using either *sick* or *ill* for the more generalized meaning.

SIDESWIPE

Dictionaries don't seem to have heard of it, but *sidewipe* was the version some editors used to demand. Apparently they were trying to lend respectability to the useful word *sideswipe*, which was originally a railroading term but contained that slangy-sounding *swipe*. The editors succeeded for a time on some newspapers, but their word has now been just about wiped out. The word for a swinging blow is *sideswipe*.

SIDEWAYS

In at least one book *sideways* is branded a corruption of *sidewise* and *endways* a corruption of *endwise*. Unadulterated nonsense. If anything, the "-ways" versions are the more dominant and their respectability was achieved four centuries ago.

SINCE

Follett notes that "there is a groundless notion current both in the lower schools and in the world of affairs that *since* has an exclusive reference to time and therefore cannot be used as a causal conjunction." The notion is indeed groundless, otherwise how explain such Shakespearean lines as, "*Since* mine own doors refuse to entertain me, I'll knock elsewhere," or "*Since* it is as it is, mend it for your own good"? The fact is that *since* in the sense of because was in use for a century before Shakespeare set quill to paper.

SLOW vs. SLOWLY   *See* ADVERBS.

SOMEPLACE   *See* ANYPLACE, SOMEPLACE.

SPEND

James Gordon Bennett the younger, who for long was the owner of *The New York Herald,* was a stickler for what he considered to be the proper use of words. Among his many dicta was one that said, "Don't say a man *spends* time; he *passes* time." It is true that the primary meaning of *spend* is to pay out, but the derived meaning of to pass, as time, has occupied a reputable place in the language since the days of Middle English. Therefore don't expend too much time worrying about Mr. Bennett's dictum.

SQUARE

There is no more reason to insist that a city square has to be square than there is to demand that a T square or an L square has to be a rectangle. Yet Bierce, in a warning about the word *square,* remarked that "a city block is seldom square." Whether you use *block* or *square* depends on where you live or work; in New York it is always *block,* except for open plazas at the intersections of two or more streets, but in Philadelphia the rectangular spaces bounded by streets are squares. Incidentally, even the legitimate New York *squares* are seldom square, but those didn't seem to bother Mr. Bierce.

STANDPOINT

Without seeming to take a position, Ayres noted that *standpoint* is "a word to which many students of English seriously object, and among them are the editors of some of our daily papers, who do not allow it to appear in their columns." Long not only took a position but also offered an explanation for it: "*Point of view* is preferable to *standpoint*; as the latter expression is logically absurd: one cannot stand on a point." The West Point cadet would be interested to learn that and so would the Senator who stands on a point of order. The point of this is that the "point" included in the word is not a physical point, much less a geometric point, which has position but no dimensions. It is usually a mental position, although it can also be a physical one, from which one views an idea or an object. The word was taken from the German *Standpunkt* more than a century ago. (All that has been said here applies also to *viewpoint*.)

STATISTIC

Resistance exists in some quarters to the word *statistic* as a false, new and unwarranted singular. False it may be, as any back-formation is. New it certainly is when compared with the similar shortened word *tactic*, which dates back to 1638. But it is hardly unwarranted, considering the wide use that is made of it by statisticians and by less specialized writers, who seem to find it needful. If you write, "To most people yesterday was unbearably hot, but to meteorologists it was just a statistic," you can't very well substitute *num-*

ber or *figure* for *statistic*. There is a shade of difference in the words; *number* or *figure* stands in isolation, whereas *statistic* is part of a pattern.

STICK (verb)

Here is a word that has almost as many informal, colloquial or slang uses as it has standard uses, and it is not always easy to distinguish between them. There is no dispute about *sticking* to one's subject or *sticking* with one's party; they are completely acceptable uses. Likewise it is all right to *stick* by a friend, though you may not, according to some authorities, *stick up* for him. The authorities are not unanimous about whether you can *stick* someone for a bill or about whether you can be *stuck* by a word in a crossword puzzle. *Stick* is almost as much of an all-purpose word as *fix*. The most that can be said about its many uses is that one by one they seem to gain respectability. Stick around for a while and maybe even *stick around* will become standard.

STOP, STAY

At least two authorities decided some years back that you don't *stop* at a hotel, you *stay* at it, because *to stop* means to cease to go forward and *to stay* means to abide, to tarry. That distinction may have been true a century ago, but it has had no validity in more recent times. Americans not only have used *stop* to mean abide but also have tacked adverbs onto it to get *stop off*, *stop over*, *stop by* and *stop in*. And this development has generated the noun *stopover*.

SUCH

The use of *such* as an adverb has aroused grammarians over the decades. Typical is this passage from Ayres: " 'I have never before seen such a large ox.' By a little transposing of the words of this sentence, we have, 'I have never before seen an ox such large,' which makes it quite clear that we should say 'so large an ox' and not 'such a large ox.' " In instances of that kind we may well bow to the strict grammarians. But there are other constructions where the adverbial-*such* idiom is so common and so natural that it would be quite unnecessary to yield to the purists. And to do so would often mean changing the word order and producing an undesired formal effect. Forget the ox for a moment and let's concentrate on girls. If we were to say, "I have never before seen *such* beautiful girls," the purists would have us change it to "girls so beautiful." But that would be tainted with stiltedness and we would be justified in ignoring the purists. The idiomatic adverbial *such* is so well entrenched that at least two of the newer dictionaries designate the word as an adverb.

SUSPECTED *See* ALLEGED.

THAT, WHO

When a newspaper reader thinks he has caught the paper in a solecism, he is sometimes insufferable. "Since when," he will write, "do you allow your reporters to say, 'As is true of many other individuals that the President has appointed . . .'? Since when is *that* rather than *who* permissible in referring to persons?" The answer, of course, is: since the language was in its infancy. Centuries ago the King James version of the Bible gave us many instances, such as, "Blessed is the man *that* sitteth not in the seat of the scornful." What critics like the newspaper reader may have caught a glint of in the dark corridors of their minds is the undisputed fact that *which* is not used to refer to a person. *That*, however, is used to refer to either persons or things. As between *who* and *that*, Fowler offers the distinction that *who* suits particular persons and *that* generic persons and he offers as examples, "You *who* are a walking dictionary," but "He is a man *that* is never at a loss."

'TIL   *See* UNTIL.

TRUCULENT

Those who maintain that the original or primary meaning of a word is the only true meaning would do well to ponder the word *truculent*. Almost every dictionary, in an unusual case of multiple blindness, defines the word as meaning savage, cruel, barbarous or something of the sort. But it is difficult to find the word used in that sense. Some authorities go on to say that it is sometimes erroneously used to mean base or mercenary. It is even more difficult to find examples of that use. American Heritage and Webster's New World, however, have seen the light. Heritage says that 86 per cent of its Usage Panel approves the "newer and milder sense synonymous with pugnacious, defiant or surly." That, of course, is just about the only sense in which the word is used these days, regardless of its derivation or original meaning.

UNDERHAND, UNDERHANDED

One book on usage says that as an adjective *underhand* is preferable to *underhanded*, although it concedes that the adverb is *underhandedly* and the noun is *underhandedness*. Oddly enough, most dictionaries, although they do not come right out and express a preference, indicate that they agree with that view since they define *underhanded* as meaning *underhand*. The explanation apparently is that *underhand* antedates *underhanded* historically, but nowadays the words are at the very least equivalent and the probability is that *underhanded* is more commonly used. Nine persons would say, "His manner was *underhanded*," to one who would use *underhand*. See -ED.

UNPRECEDENTED
If the mayor of Limping Horse, Wyoming, stands on his head for fifteen minutes to boom a charity campaign, some devotee of the gee-whiz school of journalism is sure to tag it *unprecedented*, only to have a newspaper reader write in the next day, saying in effect, "Pshaw, when I was a kid in Czechoslovakia the mayor of Krakup did that." The older the world gets the less likelihood there is that a given event is unprecedented. Does that mean that an editor should put a rigid ban on the word and threaten to tar, feather, draw and quarter any reporter using it, as one editor of a metropolitan paper did? The answer is no. All that any editor should do is demand that a reporter make a careful check and be sure he is right before he uses the word. Obviously it is a word to be employed cautiously.

UNTIL
The general tendency is to think that *until* can be used indiscriminately in the sense of up to the time that. However, caution is required in one context: When *until* follows a negative statement it implies a reversal at the time expressed. For instance, if it is stated that "He never even looked at another girl *until* he married Jane," the implication is that he began to look then. The use of the word can become ridiculous if it occurs in a statement such as, "He took no active part in the business *until* he died."

While the subject of *until* is before the house, let it be said that *till* is a perfectly good word meaning the same thing. Therefore, the contraction *'til* is superfluous and unrecognized in good usage. *See also* 'ROUND.

UPWARD OF *See* OVER.

VERBAL

Regrettably, *verbal*, which means in the form of words, has invaded the territory of *oral*, which means in the form of spoken words. It would be well if writers kept the two meanings distinct. But there are rare occasions when *verbal* can be used to encompass both meanings. For instance: "In contrast with yesterday's fistfights and rioting, today's demonstration was completely verbal, taking the form of speeches and petitions."

VIEWPOINT *See* STANDPOINT.

WANT, WISH

A species of misguided overrefinement impels some pedants to assert that one should not say, "Do you *want* your Scotch straight?" but rather "Do you *wish* your Scotch straight?" Apparently they base this preference on the fact that *want* derives from an Old Norse word meaning to lack. But the sense of wish or desire is centuries old. What is to be avoided is the phrase *want for* except where the meaning is have need, as it is in "He does not *want for* wealth."

WAY

Used as an adverb ("He is *way* behind in his work") the word has not quite become standard, yet is so close to it that a writer who uses it can hardly be faulted. So common is the word—at least in spoken language—that the accepted word, *away*, sounds unusual in some contexts such as, "In the field of moon exploration the United States is *away* ahead of Russia." Of course, *far* is a more acceptable synonym.

WEAVED, WOVE

The usual past tense of *weave* is *wove*, and the participle *woven*. Usual but not invariable. When the word is used to mean to make a path or to move from side to side, the past and participle forms are *weaved*. Therefore, one says, "The car *weaved* swiftly through the traffic," "The boxer *weaved* steadily toward his opponent" and "After the halfback had *weaved* forty yards down the field he was dropped just short of the goal line." Have we woven a tangled web?

WET, WETTED *See* BET, BETTED.

WHILE

By its very derivation *while* is related to the notion of time and some authorities demand that it be used only in contexts in which a time relationship is present. ("The sentry stood watch *while* the other soldiers slept.") Still, as an adversative conjunction it has long had the sanctioned meaning of *whereas* or *but* ("The Russians had nuclear devices, *while* their neighbors had only conventional arms") and the sanctioned meaning of *although* ("While force is outlawed in general, it is sanctioned as a means of self-defense"). Less acceptable is the use of *while* in the mere sense of *and* ("The French flag is blue, white and red, *while* the Italian flag is green, white and red"). The thing to watch out for, even in the sanctioned uses, is ambiguity ("While he had his full strength he was reluctant to use it").

WHOSE

Many teachers have maintained that *whose* could refer only to animate things. But they were too dogmatic. Common sense, as well as long usage, permits the employment of *whose* to refer to inanimate things, too. Yes, it is common sense to avoid the tortured cumbersomeness of a sentence such as this: "The new law, the durability, the value and indeed the constitutionality of which are in doubt, was applied for the first time." Is it not common sense to say, "The new law, *whose* durability, etc."? No one who uses *whose* in that way intends to show any disrespect for grammatical laws; the point is that the framers of the laws neglected to give us a genitive case for *which*.

WIDOWHOOD

Three stages of this word may be noted. Stage 1: Ayres (1882) says there is good authority for using the word in speaking of men as well as of women (and the OED in general concurs). Stage 2: Webster II (1959) defines the word as state of being a widow or, Rare, a widower. Stage 3: Webster III (1961) says it means the quality or state of being a widow; period. And that's where it stands; a man does not go through *widowhood* these days.

WORSEN

As a word that has undergone a kind of reincarnation, the verb *worsen* has suffered a little from the fact that some pedants have not been aware of the reincarnation. Centuries ago it was a standard word. Then it dropped out of good literary use, but persisted in dialectal use. The common people apparently did not know about or understandably did not like *deteriorate* and presumably saw no point in using two words, such as *get worse* or *become worse*, when one would do. As they continued to say that "Brother Ethelbert's condition has *worsened*," respected writers took the word up again in the early 1800's. It is still up.

Syntax Scarecrows

DEAR MISS THISTLEBOTTOM:

It is unnecessary for me to tell you that the word *syntax* denotes the arranging of words in a regularized way. The word itself derives from Greek roots meaning to put together in an orderly manner. If a regularized way exists, if there is an accepted order, the presumption is strong that there are rules. Oddly enough, some linguists dispute this point, maintaining that there are no rules but only what people customarily say. The difficulty here is that the linguists assume that "rules" denotes a pre-fixed code handed down from some linguistic Sinai. But rules do not have to be arbitrary or divinely transmitted; they can be, and as a matter of fact are, derived from long-established custom. To say that there are no rules is absurd. Most certainly there is a rule that demands a plural verb after a plural subject. The rule does not permit us to say, "John and Mary was married yesterday." Most certainly there is a rule that demands a past tense verb in a statement referring to the past. We may not say, "John and Mary look happy at their wedding yesterday." The only exceptions to the rules of syntax are those contained in idioms, and the fact that we know they are exceptions is the best indication that there are rules.

Those disputatious linguists are on solid ground when they say that usage modifies rules. Such modification accounts for the fact that we no longer find it necessary to have complicated inflections of nouns and adjectives or fussy indications of gender such as prevailed in Old English. But let it be noted that those modifications did not occur between Tuesday and the following Saturday.

What may be legitimately resisted are, first, the assumption that if a thousand illiterates utter a certain locution over a period of two years that locution becomes a rule of English and, second, the presumption of grammatical authoritarians that they can draw upon prejudices or illogical fantasies to lay down arbitrary rules.

It is the second piece of irrationality that I am chiefly concerned with here, Miss Thistlebottom. The split-infinitive scarecrow fits into this category and so do the "as follow" superstition and the double-genitive fetish and a dozen other specters that I have collected in this letter for your consideration. Again I do not mean to convict you of all these offenses or even of a major part of them; most of them were committed before you were born. But you did have a small part in perpetuating them and I now hope to make you see the error of your ways. Fair enough?

Yrs., etc.

ABSOLUTE PARTICIPLES *See* DANGLING AND NON-DANGLING PARTICIPLES.

AGENDA
Though technically plural, *agenda* is now thoroughly established by usage as a singular noun, meaning not things to be done but rather a list of things to be done. One piece of evidence that it is established is the fact that it has developed its own English plural—*agendas*. An additional piece of evidence is that the use of its Latin singular—agendum—is regarded as pedantic. If the singular is required, it usually takes the form "one item on the agenda" or "one entry on the agenda."

Data in one respect has followed a similar course; its singular form, *datum*, is scarcely ever used but rather is replaced by "one item in the data" or "one of the data." In another respect, however, it has followed a divergent course; it is properly, though not unexceptionally, construed as a plural: "The data are convincing." Moreover, unlike *agenda* it has not developed a piggyback plural of its own.

ALL OF
The use of the word *of* after *all* has for some time offended certain authoritarians, among them one who argued that "the words are contradictory: an entire thing cannot be of itself." To which Evans has replied that "it is hard to see why this is any more illogical than treating *none* as a part." One might go further in countering the authoritarian. Would he apply the same logic to equivalents of *all*,

[89]

such as *the whole* or *one hundred per cent?* If so, he presumably would have us say, "the whole English literature," or "one hundred per cent the tax revenues." Moreover, the *of* cannot be omitted when *all* is followed by a pronoun; one cannot say, "all us," or "all it," or "all them" or "all whom." Anyone who wishes to omit *of* after *all* (except when a pronoun follows) is free to do so if he thinks it is an unnecessary word—he may quite properly write "all the children"—but he is not free to proclaim that the law is exclusively on his side.

All the foregoing applies also to *both of.* One may say either "both of the children" or "both the children" or "both children," but not "both them."

AND ALSO
Newspaper copy editors are the thriftiest people. They are always trying to save a word here or a word there. And with good reason, because the deletion of one word may save an entire line of type at the end of the paragraph and those saved lines can mount up to a substantial chunk of badly needed space. Therefore if they wish to strike out the *and* in *and also* to save space, no one will gainsay them. But if they proclaim that they are doing it to remove a repetition, they will get an argument. *And* is merely a joining word equivalent to *plus,* but *also* is an adverb expressing some degree of similarity, equivalent to *likewise.* Thus, it is proper to write, "He is the captain of the team and also its star player." The *and also* may represent a superfluity but not a repetition.

See ALSO *under Spooks of Style.*

AND? OR?
The sentence read, "Nursing-home care was proposed for

those 65 years of age and older," and a reader took pen in hand to question the word *and*. "Would it not be more accurate," he wrote, "to say '65 years of age *or* older'?" His point, he said, was that the same people cannot be sixty-five "and older." On the other hand when the same kind of analysis is applied to the suggested correction it is evident that the same people cannot be sixty-five "or older" either; they are one or the other. However, both analyses are fallacious. What we are dealing with here is simply an ellipsis: "those 65 years of age and (those who are) older." Any more hairs that need splitting?

AS . . . AS, SO . . . AS

The rule laid down by some grammarians is that *as . . . as* is to be used in affirmative statements ("She is *as* beautiful *as* her mother") and *so . . . as* in negative statements ("She is not *so* beautiful *as* her mother"). A study reported by Bryant CAU indicates that this rule may have been followed in the middle of the last century but that the situation is quite different today. In other words, if there ever was a rule, there is none now; both combinations are used and *as . . . as* is by far the more common. One context in which *so* is used in negative statements is the disparaging colloquialism: "She's not so hot," "The movie was not so good."

AS FOLLOW, AS FOLLOWS

Some there are who insist that when a plural subject is involved the phrase must be *as follow*. They would have us write, "The provisions of the new tax bill are *as follow:*" However, they are wrong, and probably show-offs, to boot. The idiom is, and has been for centuries, *as follows* regardless of the number of the subject. We are free to suppose that the idiom arose from an ellipsis: *as* is set forth in the listing (or the account or the episode or whatnot) that *follows*. The word *follows* bears no grammatical relationship to the main subject. The *as follow* advocates, like the *between you and I* practitioners, are guilty of overrefinement, the failing that causes the girl aspiring to social grace to tackle her olive with a fork.

AS FOR

Bierce wrote: " '*As for* me, I am well,' Say, *as to* me." No grammatical reason offered, no historical basis set forth. Nothing. Actually, *as for* has been in reputable use since the days of Shakespeare and King James, and in many instances today it is the more natural of the two locutions. Can you stretch your imagination far enough to conceive of a domestic argument in which the woman of the house says, "And *as to* that good-for-nothing father of yours . . ."?

AS IF, AS THOUGH

As if makes sense. In the sentence "He acts as if he were crazy" it is simple enough to supply the ellipsis and find that the sentence is actually saying, "He acts *as* he would *if* he were crazy." But some perfectionists balk at *as though*. It seems to make no sense to say, "He acts *as* he would *though* he were crazy." All becomes clear, however, when it is realized that a now-obsolete meaning of though is *if*, and the idiom *as though* stands on a par with *as if*.

Partridge, while not disputing the validity of both forms, wonders whether they should not be differentiated. He suggests that *as though* emphasizes similarity or implies comparison and gives this example: "He reprimanded me, as though it were my fault." To him, *as if* emphasizes or implies contingency or a condition: "He reprimanded me severely. As if it were *my* fault!" Get it? No? Then forget it, and simply use the two phrases interchangeably.

For the form of the verb to be used after these idioms, see IF WITH SUBJUNCTIVE.

BACK OF, IN BACK OF

The British give the back of their hands to both these expressions. Americans tend to accept both of them, though there is less enthusiasm for *back of* than for *in back of* as in "He drove most of the distance back of (in back of) a big truck." Both are standard in American speech and are swiftly becoming so in American writing. Still, *behind* is better than either of them and more economical.

BOTH OF *See* ALL OF.

BUT: PREPOSITION OR CONJUNCTION?

Some teachers insist on regarding *but* as a conjunction ("Everyone but he laughed at the quip"); others insist on regarding it as a preposition ("Everyone but him laughed at the quip"). Neither group is wrong. What, then, is one to do? Here are two guides that should be safe: 1. If the pronoun is at the end of the sentence, regard *but* as a preposition and put the pronoun in the objective case ("Everyone laughed at the quip but him"). Not only is this grammatically acceptable, but in addition it sounds inoffensive since normally a noun at the end of a sentence is in the objective case. 2. If the pronoun appears elsewhere in the sentence, put the pronoun in the same case as the noun to which it is linked by the *but* ("Everyone but he laughed at the quip"; "The quip, directed at no one but him, fell flat").

COLLIDE

Among a dwindling number of newspapermen there is a notion that you must not say, "The car *collided* with the truck," but rather should phrase it, "The car and the truck were *in collision*." Some overcautious and undereducated lawyer must be at the bottom of this. He probably told a less-than-skeptical editor that the *collided with* version bears the taint of libel because it suggests that the car was at fault. But the derivation and meaning of the word nullify such a notion. *Collide* derives from Latin *com* (*col*), meaning together, and *laedere*, meaning to strike; the word means to strike against each other. Thus it always involves a reciprocal action. If a car *collides* with a truck, the truck simultaneously *collides* with the car. One or the other may be at fault, but nothing in the word assigns the blame.

Incidentally, it is no superstition to affirm that a collision means a coming together and hence that both objects must be in motion. Thus, Webster III's quotation (unattributed)—"waves *colliding* with the rocks"—is not a precise use of the word.

COMPOUND SUBJECTS

Normally a subject made up of more than one element takes a plural verb ("The President and Congress *are* at loggerheads"), although occasionally, when the elements add up to the same idea, the verb is singular ("The wear and tear on the car *was* tremendous"). But focus an eye on these compound subjects followed by singular verbs, all of which are correct:

Everything in the cupboard and everything on the table was *smashed.*
Everybody favoring the plan and everybody leaning toward it was *interviewed.*

> *Nobody in my house and nobody on my street* has *been robbed.*
>
> *Anyone who has read the book and anyone who has even heard of its ideas* agrees *with the author.*

Strange, eh? At first glance you might think that the explanation lies in the stress on the singular elements: *everything, everybody, nobody, anyone.* But that would not work for the following sentence, which also stresses the singular: "One Democrat and one Republican *were* named to the committee."

The true explanation would seem to be that in each instance the second "particularizer" is superfluous and has no grammatical effect; it could just as well be omitted, and in some of the instances the *and* would change to an *or*: "Everything in the cupboard and on the table was smashed"; "Everybody favoring the plan or leaning toward it was interviewed."

An odd quirk that proves nothing aside from the fact that some rules do have exceptions.

COUPLE

Here and there across the country are editors who insist that *couple* must be singular. Sometimes, to be sure, it is: "The Oswego couple was adjudged the winner of the dance contest." More often, however, you run into trouble if you demand that the word always be regarded as a singular noun. For instance, it is nonsense to write, "The couple was living in separate apartments." A more common booby-trap is the newspaper sentence that goes, "The couple was injured when their car ran off the road." You can't have it both ways; you can't regard *couple* as singular in one part of the sentence and then decide it is plural in another part. Nor, if you decide it is singular, can you write "The couple was injured when its car ran off the road." In nine cases out of nine and a half you will be safe if you consider *couple* to be plural.

DANGLING AND NONDANGLING PARTICIPLES

Genuine danglers follow this pattern: "Barking all the way, she led her dog down the street." The modifying participial phrase is out of contact with the noun it modifies (*dog*) and in contact with a noun it does not modify (*she*). The results of this solecism range from puzzlement through incongruity to hilarity.

Apparent but nongenuine danglers seem to be in this same pattern, but really are not. Still there are some purists who stand poised to pounce on them as if they were genuine. Here's an example of the nongenuine variety: "Speaking of suspicion, my wife even has my bed bugged." Participial phrases of this kind, unconnected with the rest of the sentences of which they are a part, are called absolute participles. They are equivalent to prepositions or prepositional phrases; in the example cited, *speaking of* is equivalent to *about* or *as to*.

The fundamental distinction between the two forms lies in the presence or absence of an agent that is related to or performing the action expressed in the participle. In the first example the agent doing the barking is *dog* and the word is misplaced in the sentence. In the second example, the writer or speaker has no agent in mind at all when he uses the phrase *speaking of suspicion* and he does not intend to suggest one. An agent may be lurking in the background so that the participial phrase is elliptical—in this instance it may be "since we were speaking of suspicion"— but the writer or speaker is probably quite unaware of it.

Most participles do not lend themselves to conversion to absolute phrases, yet the list of those that do has grown slowly. Some, like the perfect participle *based* in the phrase *based on* have raised sporadic objections. Others, like *owing* in the phrase *owing to*, we scarcely think of as participles any longer; indeed, Webster III designates the phrase a preposition. An incomplete list of the more common absolute participles follows:

according	*failing*
acknowledging	*following*
admitting	*given*
assuming	*granting (granted)*
barring	*including*
based	*judging*
beginning	*owing*
conceding	*providing (provided)*
concerning	*reckoning*
considering	*recognizing*
depending	*regarding*
excepting	*speaking*
excluding	*taking (one thing with another)*
	viewing

Other participles are occasionally used in absolute constructions, but they might be challenged by strict grammarians. For instance, "Looking at the dispute impartially, Jones clearly had the better case." Or, "Facing north, the ocean can be seen clearly." A borderline will always be mighty thin.

DATA *See* AGENDA.

DIFFERENT FROM, DIFFERENT THAN
It is not going to be contended here that teachers have been wrong in insisting that *different from* is inscribed in granite somewhere and brooks no chiseling or cutting of

corners. It is going to be contended, however, that one of these days we will all have to start relaxing. Usage by educated speakers and writers is beginning to erode that granite, and the first thing you know exceptions to the rule will be fully accepted. *Different from* is normal, standard grammar, and when the words are followed by a noun or pronoun there should be no tolerance of deviation: "Women are *different from* men"; "Her background is *different from* mine." Exceptions are becoming acceptable, however, when what follows is a clause, expressed or elliptical, and when (now mark this) the use of *different from* would entail a cumbersome, awkward construction. Example: "The feeling of weightlessness affected him this time in a *different* way *than* ever before." To insist on *from* would produce some such clumsy locution as, "The feeling of weightlessness affected him this time in a *different* way *from* the way it ever before had." In such situations—but only in such situations—*different than* is undoubtedly making the grade, though the grade is uphill and steep.

DOUBLE GENITIVE

Not infrequently someone questions a construction that reads like this: "He is a political associate of the President's." Since the *of* indicates the possessive (genitive), the someone argues, why tack on another possessive in the form of " 's"? Grammarians differ as to the origin and explanation of the construction, but they do not question its well-established legitimacy. One explanation is attempted by *Harper's English Grammar*, which says by way of accounting for "a poem of Wordsworth's" that "the plural of the first noun is understood after the inflected possessive, as 'a poem of (among) Wordsworth's poems . . .'" Fowler demolished that explanation some years back by observing that the phrase "that long nose of his" surely did not mean "among his noses." Jespersen offers a better explanation. He suggests that *of* in these instances is simply a grammatical device or "an empty word," which may be regarded as meaning "who is" or "which is." The device, he says, makes it possible to join words that it is difficult or impossible to join otherwise.

Curme professes to see in the double genitive "liveliness of feeling, expressing the idea of approbation, praise, censure, pleasure, displeasure: 'this appropriate remark of Mrs. Smith's,' 'that really beautiful speech of your wife's,' 'that ugly remark of her father's,' etc." Partridge suggests that the double genitive connotes familiarity in speech, citing "a friend of Bill Brown's," whereas the absence of the double genitive connotes dignity, as in "a friend of the King." It may be added that often there is a faint difference in meaning between the two constructions. When you say, "Jones is a friend of the President," you are rather looking at the matter from Jones's point of view; when you say, "Jones is a friend of the President's," you are looking at it from the President's point of view, you are stating that Jones is among his friends. Far less often there is a pronounced difference in meaning: "That picture of Smith" is quite different from "That picture of Smith's."

Semifinally, when a pronoun is involved, the possessive case is invariable: "Dick is a friend of hers," not "Dick is a friend of her."

Finally, despite the not infrequent questions that are raised, the double genitive is of long standing, idiomatic, useful and here to stay.

DOUBLE NEGATIVE

Probably no teachers are around any more who would maintain that two negatives make an affirmative, but some of their former pupils may be maintaining it. For their benefit let it be said that the maintenance is faulty. Surely when a kid says, "I don't want no more oatmeal," no affirmative statement is being made or intended. The meaning is quite negative and it shines clearly through the vulgar syntax. Another class of double negatives involves their deliberate and proper use to express what is at best a feeble affirmative—a kind of litotes, or understatement. An example of this is, "Smoking cannot be considered unharmful to health." That is not what one would consider a smashingly positive statement; it does not quite come right out and say that smoking is harmful to health. Some grammarians cite still another type of sentence that they argue constitutes a double negative though they do not condemn it or contend it makes an affirmative. Here is an example: "He could not learn to spell, not even when he received private tutoring." However, that is not really a double negative; the clause beginning "not even" is a separate thought that is part of the sentence almost through an accident of punctuation. This becomes evident if you try to invert the sentence: "Not even when he received private tutoring could he not learn to spell." Clearly the "not even" clause in the original is an independent thought tacked on for emphasis.

DROWNED *See* GRADUATED.

EACH OTHER vs. ONE ANOTHER

Many of us were taught that *each other* is used for two and *one another* for more than two. And many of us tend to agree with that dictum not only because it was drilled into us but also because of the logic of it. The indefiniteness of *another* suggests that it refers not to the second of two but rather to an additional one out of any number. Logic is not always the controlling factor in language, however, and it is indisputable that many reputable writers and speakers use *one another* to refer to only two. Usage, after all, is a reflection of what reputable users of the language actually do. Therefore we must accept *one another* as applying to two, as well as to more than two. It is more difficult to accept *each other* as applying to more than two, though it is not incorrect, but fortunately most good writers and speakers find it difficult, too.

EITHER, NEITHER—HOW MANY ALTERNATIVES?

There are those who contend that *either* and *neither* cannot be used to apply to more than two alternatives (those same people are squirming at this point because they also think there cannot be more than two alternatives, but they should see the entry ALTERNATIVES in the Witchcraft in Words section). In general those contenders are right, especially when *either* or *neither* is a pronoun or an adjective. When the words are used as conjunctions, however, the presence of three or more things is not uncommon: "Neither you nor the chairman nor the entire company is going to stop me from doing my duty as I see it." Shakespeare made no bones about using such constructions: "For I have neither wit nor words, nor worth, action, nor utterance, nor the power of speech to stir men's blood." And, of course, there is the familiar phrase "neither fish, nor flesh, nor good red herring."

EROTICA

The headline read, "Times Square Finds Erotica Has Impact," and the reader who clipped it and sent it to the editor flanked the word "Has" with exclamation points. No comment—just the exclamation points. But his meaning was clear enough: Since when, he was obviously saying, is *erotica* a singular noun? True enough, Webster II, Webster

III and the American Heritage Dictionary all designate the word as a plural noun. The Random House is silent on the subject except to note that the word is derived from a Greek plural. Webster's New World, however, says that it is "n. pl. (often with sing. v.)." That word "often" may even be an understatement; *erotica* probably appears more often as a singular noun than as a plural noun. It is doubtful whether anyone using it as a singular can be faulted. For the record, the Greek singular form of the word is *erotikos*. Ever see that used? *See* AGENDA.

FALSE PASSIVE

The so-called false passive is a false alarm. Bierce, who was an influential proponent in this country of the proscription against it, had a way of turning in alarms when there wasn't even smoke, much less fire. Here is the way he put his case:

> *"The soldier was given a rifle." What was given is the rifle, not the soldier. "The house was given a coat (coating) of paint." Nothing can be "given" anything.*

Nothing, that is, except Bierce, who can be given the back of one's hand. But that was not always true. Oddly enough, the taboo was picked up unquestioningly by newspaper editors, some of whom cling to it to this day, and it even found its way into at least one grammar book, which clothed it in impressive syntactical terms as follows:

> *When a sentence in the active form contains both an indirect and a direct object, mistakes are often made in giving the passive construction. Many times the indirect object in the active form is used as the subject in*

the passive form, but this makes an incorrect construc-
tion known as the false passive.
—Elements of English Composition, *in the Interna-*
tional Library of Technology, Scranton, Interna-
*tional Textbook Company, 1923, page 86.**

There can be no doubt that grammarians of the nine-teenth century opposed the "false passive" construction. The reason probably was, as Jespersen suggests, that they "could not class it according to their preconceived (Latin) ideas." Bryant also speaks of such a complication for the grammarian, saying: "The meaning of *I was given a chair* and *A chair was given me* was the same and he could not ex-plain the construction logically. After generations of con-demnation by the textbook writers, a name *retained object* was applied to the complement after the passive verb, and today there is little objection to the passive constructions."

Jespersen goes further and says that "the new construc-tion with the indirect object made the subject of the pas-sive, while producing no ambiguities or other inconven-iences worth mentioning, increases the ease and freedom of the language and adds considerably to its stylistic re-sources . . ."

Is it too much to hope that the "was given" taboo has been given a decent burial?

FUSED PARTICIPLE *See* GENITIVE WITH GERUND.

GENITIVE WITH GERUND

Fowler, a learned moderate who has been a respected guide in matters of usage since the 1920's, inveighed against

---

* Let me rush at once to the confessional to acknowledge that in the first edition (1933) of a journalism text, *Headlines and Deadlines,* Robert E. Garst and I made this same point, but after we learned better we ex-purgated it.

fetishes and superstitions, yet on rare occasions wore a bear's tooth around his own neck. One such was his insistence on avoiding what he called the fused participle: Don't write, "I hate him getting all the credit," but rather, "I hate his getting all the credit." There is no doubt that what might be termed natural expression calls for *his* instead of *him*; the gerund is normally preceded by a genitive. At the same time it must be acknowledged that there are situations in which the use of the genitive is not feasible. Fowler himself inadvertently disclosed a couple. In the clause "Which will result in many having to go into lodgings" he suggested making it *many's*, and in the sentence "It is no longer thought to be the proper scientific attitude to deny the possibility of anything happening" he favored altering it to *anything's*. The suggested changes can hardly be called English, to use Dr. C. T. Onions's characterization. The conclusion is that although normally the gerund should be preceded by a genitive, there are instances that call for exceptions. One would be a sentence in which the idiomatic sound would be violated; "The town was captured without a shot being fired." Another would be a sentence containing a noun or pronoun that has no commonly recognized possessive form: "There are long odds against that happening." A third would be a sentence containing a long phrase for which a possessive form cannot be contrived: "Imagine children as young as twelve years old being haled into court!"

GENITIVE WITH INANIMATE NOUNS

The rule is . . . no; the custom has always been (that's better) . . . to use the *'s* genitive with nouns representing animate beings and an *of* phrase with nouns representing things. However . . .

Jespersen lists these exceptions:

Before sake (*"for pity's sake," "for argument's sake," "for old time's sake"*).

In some *"more or less fixed phrases"* (*"at death's door," "my mind's eye," "out of harm's way"*). This category also includes the genitive of ship, boat and vessel as in *"the ship's provisions," "the boat's crew," "the vessel's keel."*

In poetry and higher literary style (*"my sweet sleep's disturbers," "in beauty's mold," "religion's tottering dome"*).

Before end (*"a rope's end," "wits' end," "journey's end"*). Also with related notions, especially with edge (*"cliff's edge," "grave's mouth," "mountain's side"*).

In indications of measure of space (*"a foot's pace," "a stone's throw," "a cow's length"*). With these, says Jespersen, should be compared such phrases as *"money's worth," "a shadow's weight."* Note also, he adds, *"a shilling's worth."*

In indications of a measure of time (*"the long day's task," "a second's pause," "a good hour's work"*). And with words denoting time where no measure is indicated (*"this evening's paper," "yesterday's rain," "tomorrow's test"*).

Bryant CAU lists the following areas of exceptions and their percentages in the 272 examples found in a study of about a thousand pages of *Life, Time, Newsweek* and *Coronet* (and let it be conceded at once that they are not the best subjects for a study of good usage):

Political, 40%: "Germany's rearming," "the nation's social security."
Physical objects, 16%: "turnpike's stations," "book's main divisions," "car's performance."

Periods of time, 14%: "four hours' ascent," "by the week's end."

Commercial products, 7%: "GM's patents," etc.

Publications, 6%: "Newsweek's article," "Time's staff."

Organizations and institutions, 5%: "Harvard's School of Public Health," "U.N.'s Korea Civil Assistance Command."

"The other 12%," says Bryant, "occurred in connection with collective nouns, as in 'the U.S. Bureau's 30-day outlook' (6%); abstract nouns, as in 'freedom's ring' (.8%); with personifications, as in 'Death's head' (.4%); and with the word 'world,' as in 'the world's greatest adventure' (5%). Another study found a total of 489 examples with a similar distribution."

What shall be said, in the light of all this, concerning the rule—pardon, the custom—about not using the 's genitive with lifeless things? At the pedantic extreme is Follett, who says: ". . . now every newspaper thinks it normal and right to speak of 'Florida's governor,' 'Berkeley's Clark Kerr,' 'the town's high school,' 'Cornell's division of Industrial Relations' and 'the nation's capital.' The truth is that these possessives in the 's form are newfangled and false." Many skilled users of English will disagree with that extreme position. A score or more years ago this statement appeared in Jespersen: "During the last few decades the genitive of lifeless things has been gaining ground in writing (especially among journalists) . . ." It cannot be denied that journalists had much to do with the spread of the usage, but it is none the less valid for that; for better or worse, journalism does influence English usage. Curme says that "This distinction between living and lifeless things is not closely observed," and he goes on to prescribe that to take the 's genitive "the thing must usually have some sort of individual life like a living being, but this idea of life may be very faint." But there are abundant instances in which the 's genitive is acceptable even though no idea of life is present: "today's paper," "the car's spark plugs," "the sun's rays," "the moon's orbit," "the company's assets." Naturally, no one in his right mind would try to convert all *of* genitives into 's genitives; no one would be likely to translate "piece of wood" into "wood's piece" or "loss of breath" into "breath's loss." On the other hand, if the purists are going to insist on their rule, perhaps we shall have to rewrite our national anthem to get rid of "dawn's early light," "twilight's last gleaming" and "rockets' red glare." Perhaps they would even like us to get rid of the word *its*.

In summary, we seem to be approaching a stage where 's genitives with lifeless things are acceptable except when they sound unusual enough or strained enough to call attention to themselves. That would rule out such a phrase as "this item's end."

GRADUATED

It is patently incorrect to say, "He graduated college." Perhaps deducing from the stricture against this locution that the student has nothing to do with the award of a diploma, some nit-pickers jumped to the conclusion that it is also incorrect to say, "He graduated from college." But they are wrong. A student can either *graduate from* or *be graduated from* a college; it depends on whether you are thinking of the student's achievement in completing his studies or the institution's magnanimity in admitting him to a degree. Actually, the form *graduated from* is by far the more common one; the OUD even designates the form *was graduated from* as "now rare exc. U.S."

Perhaps arising from the misapprehension about the verb

graduate, a similar one concerns the verb *drown*. I have heard of editors who forbid their underlings to write, "He *drowned* in the river," and insist that they make it, "He was *drowned* in the river." They may be correct in their insistence if a gang of racketeers had something to do with the untimely demise, but not otherwise. Fortunately, the misapprehension does not seem to be widespread.

HAD BETTER, HAD RATHER

On the one hand, Bierce will tell you that these phrases result from what he calls the erroneous restoring of such contractions as *he'd* for *he would* and *I'd* for *I would*, "producing such monstrosities as 'He had better beware,' 'I had better go.'" On the other, and far more knowledgeable, hand, Greenough observes that *I had, we had*, etc., were contracted to *I'd, we'd*, etc., "and many persons suppose that *I had* . . . is a mistaken expansion of *I'd* (the contraction of *I would*)." In other words, it all depends on which is the original: *had* or *would*. The evidence is unmistakable that the *had* phrase was the original idiom. It goes at least as far back as Chaucer: "I hadde levere than my Scherte/ That ye hadde rad his legende, as have I." Thus, far from ruling out *had better* and *had rather*, you had better give them the preference; they are unexceptionable. And you can bet your Scherte on that.

HAVE, "CAUSATIVE"

The verb *have* followed by a passive perfect participle gives rise to one construction that everyone finds blameless ("I *had* a tooth *pulled* this morning") and another that some people regard as a solecism ("I *had* my jaw *broken* this morning"). In the first construction the *have* is regarded as causative, indicating volition. In the second the solecism-searchers still regard the *have* as causative and thus find the sentence idiotic: The speaker wouldn't deliberately cause his own jaw to be broken, would he? The trouble is not with the sentence but rather with the objectors. They overlook the fact that the auxiliary *have* is not invariably causative. It has other meanings, one of which is given in Webster II as "to suffer or experience from an exterior source." (Oddly, the extra-permissive Webster III gives no definition that quite encompasses the exterior-source notion and no example that illustrates it, but the relatively conservative Webster II not only gives the explicit definition but in addition offers the illustration "He *had* his leg *broken.*") Lest it be thought that this noncausative use is a latter-day debasement of the language, let it be noted that Shakespeare had Falstaff say, "The other night I fell asleep here behind the arras, and had my pocket picked . . ." and Dickens wrote in *David Copperfield*, "King Charles the First had his head cut off." Just as acceptable are today's sentences: "Employes who fail to work the full eight hours will have their pay reduced proportionately" or "A boy and a girl student had their hair singed by lighted matches thrown at them by other students." There is no need to recast those sentences; they are perfectly good as they stand.

-ICS WORDS

Is *politics* always singular? The answer is no, although it is singular most of the time. When -*ics* words are used to refer to a subject, a science, a profession or a system they are construed as singular nouns: "International *politics* was taught at the university." But when such words are used to refer to practical activities or qualities they are sometimes construed as plurals: "His *politics* were successful in getting the bill approved." Here are two more contrasting examples: "Acoustics is not an exact science"; "The acoustics of the new auditorium are deplorable."

IF WITH SUBJUNCTIVE

Many teachers have been laying down a flat rule that *if* should be followed by a verb in the subjunctive mood, but the rule is too flat. *If* takes the subjunctive when it introduces a clause containing a condition that is not true or that is merely hypothetical ("If I were you," "If man should one day be able to control his blood pressure, his life span might be measurably increased"). Often, however, *if* serves other purposes. It may introduce a clause of concession ("If it hurts, I will let you know"). It may introduce a clause stating a flat condition ("If a driver goes eighty miles an hour, he is liable to a fine"). Or it may, as a synonym for *whether* (*see* IF, WHETHER, *in the Words section*), merely introduce an indirect question ("The defense counsel asked the witness if he was a paid agent of Moscow"). In all these instances the straight indicative mood rather than the subjunctive is indicated. Pence offers a practical rule to decide when to use the subjunctive and when the indicative: If the emphasis is on the *if*, the subjunctive is to be preferred ("If he were innocent, he would not have been convicted by the jury"); if the emphasis is on the statement following the *if*, the indicative is to be preferred ("If he is innocent, let's stand by him").

IT'S ME

If someone were to show an English teacher a picture of her class at school and ask if she could pick out Chaim Perez, it is reasonably certain she would not say, "That's him in the center." She would surely say, "That's he in the center." But when it comes to the first person pronoun, one wonders. If someone asked her who was standing in the last row, is it not possible she would say, "That's me"? Forty years ago C. T. Onions said that *it is me* was "used even by educated speakers" and a decade later Sterling A. Leonard wrote that the *me* was established in usage, although both writers found the use of the objective case of the third person pronouns (*him, her, us*) either vulgar or dubious. (See *Modern English and Its Heritage*, Margaret M. Bryant.) Although the *It is me* construction is certainly gaining, at least in spoken language, one should not be as confident today as those writers were thirty and forty years ago that the *me* is established usage.

The *him* construction is quite dubious. I often listen, in season, to telecasts of the New York Mets games and I have noted, not without appreciation, that one of the Mets announcers, Lindsey Nelson, will report that Chuck Smith is being inserted as a pinch hitter and an instant later say, "That's he now, swinging the big bat." That seems to suggest that the *him* construction is not altogether established.

When somebody gets me on the phone and says, "Mr. Bernstein, please," I panic. I can't possibly say, "This is him," and I feel like an affected ass saying, "This is he." Each time I resolve that in the future I will say, "Speaking," but the next time such a call comes I find myself sounding like an affected ass. The practical, if not linguistic, solution is, I suppose, to follow the advice of the telephone company and say, "Good morning, Bernstein speaking. May I help you?"

NONE

For a long, long time teachers have been frightening us by telling us never to use *none* as a plural; the word was a contraction of *not one,* and that was that. What they were doing, one suspects, was carrying out the pedagogical technique of laying down a rule rather than allowing leeway for uncertain individual judgments. However, *none* sometimes means *not one* and sometimes means *not any* or *no amount*, and it is more commonly construed as a plural than as a singular. When the singular idea predominates—that is, when the word truly suggests *not one*—the verb is indeed singular: "The three towns all have high tax rates, but *none has* its own police force." Likewise, when *none* is followed by a singular noun it is usually construed as a singular, as in "*None* of the dinner *was* fit to eat" or "*None* of the work *was* finished in time." But there are exceptions to this, too: "*None* of the audience *were* enthusiastic about the play," "*None* of the company's personnel *were* on the picket line." It should be apparent that a flat rule is not advisable. But most often the singular sounds pedantic and the plural is called for: "*None* of the boys *were* to blame," "*None* of the books *were* interesting," "*None* of the enemy *were* captured."

NUMBER

Some people are very literal-minded about the question of grammatical number; they tend to concentrate on the exact word that they take to be the subject of the sentence, when sometimes they should be looking at the thought that the word or words represent. A woman wrote to criticize a newspaper sentence that read, "A growing number of Germans think there should be more uniformity in their language." In effect standing over us brandishing a ruler, she wrote: "A number (singular) thinks. Numbers (plural) think." That was, presumably, our lesson for the day. Wresting the ruler from her hand, the answering letter told her that although *number* was indeed a singular noun, *a number of* was equivalent to *many* or *some*. The reply went on to tell her that a good rule of thumb was that *the number* takes a singular verb but *a number* takes a plural verb.

And the same rule of thumb applies to similar words, like *variety* and *total*. "The *total* of unemployed in the town *is* 31,562," but, "A *total* of 31,562 *are* unemployed in the town." And "*The variety* of birds in the wildlife refuge *is* remarkable," but, "A *variety* of birds *are* found in the wildlife refuge." The phrase *a total of* is far from being the true subject of its sentence; it is equivalent to a speaker's "er" or a pianist's vamp till ready. Most often it is used because the writer either does not wish to begin the sentence with a numeral or rightly rejects beginning it with a clumsy spelling out of the figure: "Thirty-one thousand five hundred sixty-two."

Mention should be made here of the question of numbers that are to be considered not as expressions of individual units but rather as expressions of an integral quantity. You would not write, "Three inches of snow have fallen," because you are not thinking of individual inches; you are thinking of a quantity of snow that accumulates to that depth. Likewise you would not write, "About $10,000 were added to the cost of the project," because again you are thinking of a sum of money, not of individual dollars.

See also COUPLE *and* NONE.

OUGHT (TO)

Webster II says: "The infinitive without *to* occurs after *ought* in older or poetic use." The implication seems to be that in newer, nonpoetic use the *to* is required. Some strict constructionists have jumped to just that conclusion, but the conclusion is too sweeping. It is true that the *to* should be inserted in a sentence such as this: "No actress ought appear nude on the stage." But its omission is perfectly correct and idiomatic in a sentence such as this: "An actress ought not appear nude on the stage." Pence and Evans explain that in negative statements the *to* is often omitted, which is true as far as it goes. To go further, however, it may be said that if any qualifier, negative or not, intervenes between the auxiliary *ought* and the main verb, the *to* may (not must) be omitted. Examples: "A sentry ought always be alert for unusual sounds." "Ideally, an airplane ought, in all kinds of weather, be able to take off and land safely." "A good Boy Scout ought at all times be prepared."

PERFECT INFINITIVE

The perfect infinitive—the one with a "have" in it—is used to denote a time that is earlier than that of the main verb of the sentence. The following sentences express two, and perhaps three, different thoughts:

1. *I should like (now) to have been (last night or a week ago) at the party.*
2. *I should have liked (last night or a week ago) to go (same level of time) to the party.*
3. *I should have liked (last night or a week ago) to have gone (the night before last? two weeks ago?) to the party.*

Conceivably situations could arise in which the third variation would be clear and sensible: Here is one: "At the Shakespeare Festival last summer I should have been happy to have been better educated in Shakespeare's plays." But in the general run of situations variations 1 and 2 are the only real alternatives, and variation 3 is disapproved. Teachers do not always explain these distinctions clearly, which accounts for this entry.

POSSESSIVE   *See* DOUBLE GENITIVE, GENITIVE WITH IN-
ANIMATE NOUNS *and* GENITIVE WITH GERUND.

POSSESSIVE WITH INANIMATE NOUNS *See* GENITIVE WITH INANIMATE NOUNS.

PRONOUN WITH POSSESSIVE ANTECEDENT

"Immediately upon the President's arrival a crowd broke into cheers for him." Most people would understand that sentence and find nothing wrong with it. But a rule enunciated by strict grammarians forbids such a construction. Harper's states the rule thus: "A pronoun cannot take as an antecedent a noun in the possessive case." A somewhat softer version appears in Follett: "A noun in the possessive case, being functionally an adjective, is seldom a competent antecedent of a pronoun." And an equally soft version is given in Pence: "A pronoun should not, as a rule, refer to a noun in the possessive case." However, what Harper's goes on to say and the others do not say is that "this rule is little respected by writers and authors—if indeed known." And that is the truth. Sir Ernest Gowers, a respected authority on English, who updated Fowler's *Modern English Usage*, goes so far in a book of his own as to correct a sentence of officialese in a way that violates the dimly perceived rule. Following is the sentence from *The Complete Plain Words*, with Gowers's suggested change parenthesized: "The examiner's search would in all cases be carried up to the date of the filing of the complete specification, and the examiner (he) need not trouble his head with the subject of disconformity." What, then, shall be concluded about the rule? Just this: The rule shall be considered valid whenever it functions to preclude ambiguity. That would make it apply to a sentence such as this: "John's roommate said he had a headache." But if there is no possibility of ambiguity and observance of the rule would serve only to gratify the strict grammarian's sense of fitness, forget it.

RATHER THAN

These words provide an example of how usage sometimes overrides grammatical theory. If *than* is a conjunction (as it is), qualified by *rather*, an adverb (which is true), then the elements joined by the conjunction should be parallel (and they usually are): "I would go naked rather than wear the new fashions"; "The city should consider relocating rather than evicting slum dwellers." However, when *rather than* acquires the stronger meaning of "to the exclusion of" in place of the meaning "in preference to" the conjunction mysteriously takes on the shading of a preposition. Hence, usage will often produce this kind of sentence: "The President's speech helps his opponents rather than supporting (grammatically *supports*) his own position"; "The crystallography indicates a double helix rather than calling (grammatically *calls*) for a single spiral." When the *rather than* comes first in the construction, this quasi-prepositional use is more common: "Rather than supporting (not *supports*) his own position, the President's speech helps his opponents."

SO   *See* VERY PLUS PARTICIPLE.

SO . . . AS   *See* AS . . . AS, SO . . . AS.

SPLIT INFINITIVE

Some teachers have scared the pants off people on the subject of the split infinitive. The dire warnings they have sounded have been so misinterpreted and misapplied that even completely innocent constructions have been convicted and tortured.

What the teachers were talking about was avoidance of splitting the *to* away from the verb as in, "He promised *to* quickly *make* his point." What they neglected to point out was that when the infinitive contains an auxiliary there is nothing amiss about dividing the auxiliary from the main verb; all authorities on usage are agreed on this point. Yet some of the terrified ex-pupils will insist on such sentences as, "He demanded fully to be briefed an hour before each committee meeting," whereas the obvious and natural construction would be, "He demanded to be fully briefed, etc."

Some even more timid souls have got the impression that even when no *to* infinitive is present, one must not split parts of a compound verb. Thus they will write, "He universally was respected," or, still worse because of ambiguity, "A plan for eliminating slums gradually has been evolving in the measures adopted by Congress." There is no rule in English that forbids separating the parts of a compound verb. Indeed, more often than not the natural position for an adverb is just ahead of the verb it modifies; hence, "has been gradually evolving."

This natural positioning of the adverb carries us to the heart of the split-infinitive issue. The question that arises is this: If we do not boggle at "He favors really getting to the bottom of it," why should we boggle at "He wants to really get to the bottom of it"? It was not always so. From about the fourteenth century on (according to Bryant) the adverb began to take its place after the *to* and ahead of the verb and was so used by good writers. But then "authoritarian grammarians of the 18th and 19th centuries . . . selected it as something to be avoided under all circumstances." Just why is not clear. But within the last few decades reputable writers have been shaking off the shackles of the authoritarians and it is a safe guess that within the near future the split-infinitive bugaboo will be finally laid to rest. Naturally, when the split involves clumsiness ("It is my purpose *to, without malice or hatred, but with a desire for doing what is right, condemn* the proposal of the Arkansas Senator") it will not be tolerated. But that will not be because it is a split infinitive but because it is a gaucherie.

SUBJECTIVE COMPLEMENT

No confusion arises concerning the subjective complement of a finite verb: It will be in the nominative case just as the subject of the verb is ("It was *he* that I saw"). Nor does confusion usually arise concerning the subjective complement after an infinitive that has a subject of its own: Both will be in the objective case ("I took the fat man to be *him*"). However, when an infinitive has no subject, the subjective complement seems to give trouble. A letter writer questioned a United States Treasury Department publication that said, "A noun or pronoun following the infinitive *to be* is in the nominative case if the infinitive has no subject," giving as an example, "He was thought to be *I*." The letter writer asked, "How can the infinitive 'to be' ever have anything but the objective case on either end?" Follett seems to have had the same misconception, for he cites (and indirectly corrects) a sentence as follows: "Our concern was to find out who we were and whom (not who) we wished to be." The correction is incorrect. Pence puts the matter succinctly in this way: "The subjective complement after an infinitive that has no grammatical subject of its own is in the nominative case; for the subject complement refers to the subject of the main verb, which is, of course, in the nominative case." Pence gives as an example, "The person was thought to be I." The directly parallel part of the Follett sentence, in its direct form, would read, "We wished to be who." What apparently led the letter writer and Follett astray is the rule that the subject of an infinitive is always in the objective case, with the corollary that if such an infinitive has a subjective complement, it, too, is in the objective case. Maybe the main point that emerges from this grammatical morass is that sometimes the United States Government is right.

THAT (conjunction)

Some newspaper offices maintain a virtual taboo against the conjunction *that*. In doing so they occasionally produce a sentence such as this: "Smilovakia has declared war on neighboring Chucklevania is unthinkable." Obviously the taboo is too far-reaching. Yet it is true that in many, many instances the conjunction is unnecessary. The tendency in this country, as contrasted with Britain, is to do without it whenever it is safe or comfortable to do so. In a short, simple, readily comprehensible sentence the word may be omitted: "He felt confident the Giants would win." But there are three situations in which omission of *that* is inadvisable. One is a sentence in which a time element intervenes between the verb and the clause. If you write, "The Premier said last week some army officers mutinied," omission of the *that* leaves ambiguity concerning whether the statement or the mutiny took place last week. A second situation calling for the conjunction is one in which the clause is in apposition to a noun: "Thirty-two Senators signed an appeal youth should be able to present its case to the nation." There it is simply a matter of smoother reading. The third situation is one that might be called the red-herring sentence, in which the verb of the clause is long delayed, putting the reader off the scent: "City Hall disclosed a report on city contracts let without competitive bidding had been leaked to a television commentator." Without a *that* after *disclosed*, the reader is not alerted to the fact that *report* is going to be the subject of a clause. Probably the only broad guide that can be issued is that in cases of doubt a *that* should be inserted. As was done in the preceding sentence.

THERE IS vs. THERE ARE

No problem concerning the number of the verb arises in this kind of sentence: "There were three chickens, a cow and a horse on the farm." However, if you put the cow or the horse at the head of the parade, an option appears. You can keep the verb plural and no one can fault you. But some writers prefer, "There was a cow, a horse and three chickens on the farm," and that is generally deemed acceptable, too, because of the proximity of a singular noun to the verb. Likewise, when the first element of the compound subject is so lengthy that the second element is far removed from the verb the singular form is quite proper: "There is also a new 'control center' instrument panel and an exclusive new Dual Comfort front seat, available on most models." If two or more elements of the subject are so closely related as to form a unit, the singular verb is definitely preferable: "In the exhibition there was the needle and thread used by Betsy Ross"; "There has been ebb and flow over the years in the court's interpretation of the doctrine."

TOO   *See* VERY PLUS PARTICIPLE.

VERY PLUS PARTICIPLE

Only a dwindling rearguard of purists would object these days to "I was very pleased" or "He was very interested." *Pleased* and *interested* are participles that have become adjectives, which can properly be qualified by *very*. But that does not mean that all participles used predicatively are adjectives, properly qualified by *very*. You cannot, for instance, say, "He was very injured." One authority tells us, "When the past participle of a verb is used as an adjective . . . it may be qualified by *very* . . ." (Evans CW). That is true. But the problem is, how do you tell when the participle is being used as an adjective? There is no infallible test, but when the verbal quality is quite clear—"The victim was slashed"—or when it is not entirely concealed— "The flight was delayed by fog"—the modifier *very* should not be used. In other words, in those circumstances the participle is not regarded as an adjective. When the participle denotes a quality or a condition, as contrasted with an action—something that happened, perhaps—we need not balk at using *very*. Otherwise, the qualifier should be *very much*.

What is true of *very* in this context applies also to the adverbs *too* and *so*.

WAS GIVEN CONSTRUCTION *See* FALSE PASSIVE.

WHETHER OR NOT

A letter writer criticized this sentence: "Whether or not it was the advertiser's intention, the TV commercial had a salutary effect on viewers." He argued that *whether or not* contained a redundancy and that the *or not* should be dropped. Usually the *or not* is superfluous, as it is in the following sentence: "It could not be ascertained *whether* the Senator's statement was true *or not*." But when the intention is to give equal stress to the alternatives, the *or not* is mandatory. And one way to test whether those two words are necessary is to substitute *if* for the *whether*. If that change results in a different meaning, the *or not* should be supplied. In the first sentence quoted above, it would alter the meaning; in the second quoted sentence it would not.

See also IF, WHETHER *in* Witchcraft in Words.

WHO, WHOM

The waves of change are washing against the pronouns *who* and *whom*. As to *who*, the day is surely coming when it will completely displace *whom* standing at the head of a

sentence or clause, whether the sentence is interrogative
("*Who* did you write to?") or declarative ("*Who* the Republicans will nominate is in doubt"; "I have no idea *who*
the Republicans will nominate"). Such a change would
seem to be inevitable not only because of a centuries-old
tendency to divest the language of inflections, especially
valueless ones, but also because of the strong urge of speakers and writers to regard the first noun in a sentence or
clause as being in the nominative case. One can be a cham-
pion of correctness in usage and still maintain that no one
should be compelled to work out an intricate puzzle to determine whether his construction is correct; correctness
should be something that is obvious instanter. One should
not have to put together a grammatical jigsaw to discover
the correctness or incorrectness of sentences like these:
"The police arrested a man *who* they said was the thief";
"The police arrested a man *whom* they identified as the
thief." The day is coming when *who* will be deemed correct
in both sentences.

When the new usage becomes established, grammarians
will not, of course, be able to explain it to pupils. They will
have to throw it into that catch-all bin labeled "idiom," just
as they have had to do with *than whom* (q.v. in Imps of
Idioms section), which is fully established but unexplain-
able.

It is not being suggested here that the word *whom* is
going to disappear altogether. It almost certainly will survive for some time in constructions in which it appears directly after a preposition—that is, in situations where its use
entails no clash with the user's instinct and no puzzle-solv-
ing procedure. No such problems are presented in constructions such as "With *whom* did you spend the night?" or
"To *whom* it may concern" or "For *whom* the bell tolls."

For the time being, the recommendation here is that

teachers go right on teaching and editors go right on demanding the distinction between *who* and *whom* because the revolution has not yet arrived. It is brewing, though, and it has been for a long time.

Imps of Idioms

DEAR MISS THISTLEBOTTOM:

As if it weren't bad enough that sticklers try to do away with all meanings of words except those that fit their own erroneous preconceptions and try to clamp their homemade straitjackets on various pieces of perfectly acceptable syntax, some of them question and try to modify long-established, well-established idioms.

Idioms, it must be remembered, are sports in the linguistic garden. Most of them are unaccountable mutations, often following no rules of logic or sense. We know perfectly well what they mean, we use them without hindrance, but we rarely examine their components to determine how it is that they convey the meaning that is universally understandable. But there are always some sticklers around who do analyze them and then, discovering that they lack logic, attempt to reconstruct them or abolish them. Occasionally a baseball player, up from the sticks, will use a completely unorthodox stance at the plate, lack a level swing at the ball, yet bat a consistent .300. No coach in his right mind would do much to try to convert him to orthodoxy; he would let well enough alone. Similarly, there must be plenty of people with an aesthetic eye who consider the Stars and Stripes to be an aesthetic abomination. Do they go around agitating to convert the flag into a red, white and blue specimen of cubism or abstract expressionism or something? Of course, they don't. But your idiom idiots do attempt things much like that. I don't mean you, Miss Thistlebottom, but I do mean those who take a look at the expression *if worst comes to worst* and say, "Ridiculous! It should be *if worse comes to worst*." More about that a little later. Right now let's take a look at a few common idioms that the sticklers, had they thought of it, would have stuck their stickpins into.

ALL OF A SUDDEN

The *all of* part may be clear enough, but what on earth is *a sudden? Sudden* a noun? The answer is yes, it is a noun but an obsolete one except in that kind of phrase. Paul Horgan, a careful writer, was apparently bothered by the idiom because in *To the Mountains* he has this sentence: "All suddenly a most childish wave of lonesomeness broke over him."

AT THAT

In a sentence such as "We'll let it go *at that*" the phrase is at least explainable: "We'll let it go at that point"—that is, we won't go any further. But how about when it means moreover or even so or however, as in such sentences as "The vacuum cleaner worked poorly and it was costly at that" or "The vacuum cleaner does a pretty good job, but at that it's too costly"? V. H. Collins in *A Book of English Idioms* says that the colloquial expression "is one of the phrases that we might well put on the list of those to be expelled from the language, and be sure it would not be missed." And Partridge in DS says it is "confusing to a foreigner" (as, by the way, a great many idioms are) and so "little used in the Dominions." Yet, meaningless or no, the phrase is understandable and it is here to stay.

BACK AND FORTH

Whatever it is that's in motion, how did it get there in

the first place so that it first comes *back* and then goes *forth?* And the same question might be asked of *hither and thither* and *hither and yon*. Much more sensible, it would seem, are phrases that describe a setting out from where we are and a returning to the same place: *to and fro, there and back*. But sensibleness and idiom are not necessarily the same thing.

BEG THE QUESTION

Nothing in the meaning of the English word *beg* affords any clue to its meaning in this phrase. The words are a translation of the Latin term in logic *petitio principii*. The meaning of the idiom is to assume as true the very point that is under discussion. Brewer (*Dictionary of Phrase and Fable*) gives this example: "To say that parallel lines will never meet because they are parallel, is simply to assume as a fact the very thing you profess to prove." Frequently, but erroneously, the phrase is used as if it meant to evade a direct answer to a question.

DEAD AS A DOORNAIL

Why a doornail? A doornail is a large-headed nail at one time used as a stud on doors, but what is so dead about it no one seems to know. Shall we then do away with the expression and cling to *dead as a herring* or *dead as Julius Caesar?* Hardly.

HAS (IS) YET TO . . .

Examine, if you please, the sentence "Jones has yet to pitch a complete game." We all grasp the sense with no difficulty whatever. But what on earth do the words actually mean? You cannot omit the *yet* and still have the intended meaning, nor can you move the word to any other position. If the sentence read "Jones has not yet pitched a complete

game," the *yet* could be omitted or could be moved. Obviously, then, in the original wording *yet* is the crucial word.
Still, no dictionary definition explains it as it is used here.
Webster III pretends to. After setting forth the definition
"up to now; so far," it gives this example: "there is ∼ to be
any scientist of any repute who encourages . . . the saucer
prophets." However, if you try to insert either of the defining phrases in place of the swung dash (∼) it won't work, it
won't make sense. But of course *yet* will. This use of *yet*
must be set down as one of the most baffling idioms in the
language, but nobody has ever questioned it.

How are you? or How do you do?

There are probably no more common idioms in English
than these, yet they hinge on a fairly uncommon meaning
of *how*. The sense of the word here is in what condition or
state. The more usual sense is in what manner or by what
means.

It goes without saying

We all know that this combination of words means that
something is so obvious that it does not need to be spoken
of, that it is self-evident. But why *goes*? The answer is that
the phrase is a translation of the French *cela va sans dire*.

So long

The label for this one must be "origin obscure." Went-
worth and Flexner's *Dictionary of American Slang* hazards
the guess that the farewell derives from the Arabic *salaam*
and the Hebrew *sholom*, both of which mean "peace." The
OUD does not agree, and Webster's New World asserts
that this is "said to be folk etymology." Partridge in DS says
"that a suggested derivation from the Hebrew *selah* (God
be with you) is not to be wholly ignored," but then in a

second thought, set forth in a 1961 Supplement, he says that the phrase "is perhaps short for 'Good-bye. So long,' elliptical for 'God be with you so long as we are apart.' " In a third thought appearing in a 1970 Supplement he thinks that derivation from the Hebrew *shalom* is "the most likely theory of all." Then again you may like Ivor Brown's suggestion (in *A Word in Edgeways*) that *so long* comes from "Good luck for so long as we are parted and until we see one another again." That is, indeed, so long! If this is to be a guessing game, let's throw another idea into the pot: Perhaps the phrase derives from "So I'll be getting along." That at least has the appropriate casual sound. It seems to be as likely a guess as the others. But the last word will have to be "origin obscure."

Something else again

What does *again* mean in this idiomatic phrase? Dictionaries are not of much help in explaining the word as used here. Webster III professes to explain it, saying it means in addition, besides, and giving the example "that's something else ∼." But does the phrase really mean *something else in addition* or *something else besides?* Rarely. The most common use is in a sentence like this: "Marijuana may be relatively harmless, but heroin is something else again." Obviously the phrase has here the meaning *something quite different* or, crudely, *something quite else.* This is not to suggest that in this combination of words *again* means quite, though that definition would come closer to the truth than what dictionaries offer.

From idioms that provoke the question "What do they mean?" it is only half a step to those that seem to contain a meaningless meaning ("send no money") or, perversely, a reverse meaning ("climb down"). These are the ones the sticklers do pounce upon. In a triumphant tone of discovery they seek to proclaim the ignorance of people who use such expressions and succeed only in betraying their own ignorance. A modest list will disclose the kind of thing they stickle about.

Yrs., etc.

ALL . . . NOT

"All women are not neat" is a fair example of the idiom questioned here. Analyzed literally, what it says is that not a woman in the world is neat. Patently that is not the intention, nor would anyone but a perverse stickler read it that way. The intended meaning is "Not all women are neat." A writer who is concerned with precision would frame the sentence that way, but he would not deny anyone the right to frame it in the illogical yet idiomatic and completely understandable fashion.

ASIDE FROM

The phrase *aside from* is tagged by the Whitford and Foster *Concise Dictionary of American Grammar and Usage* as colloquial. The Random House labels it U.S. Informal, but some other dictionaries accept it as standard. The latter verdict would seem to be proper. The phrase is used without qualm by reputable writers.

BABY-SITTER

What is a *baby-sitter*, anyhow? One who sits a baby? One who sits on a baby? It is true that compounds normally should not be formed in this way—that is, by omitting a preposition that is an intimate part of the phrase. Thus, we should not speak of a laurel-rester (one who rests *on* his laurels) or of a hip-shooter (one who shoots *from* the hip). But baby-sitter came quickly into common use without the slightest competition from any such thing as *baby-watcher* or *baby mate* and it is now a well-established idiom.

[131]

BEST FOOT FORWARD

Anyone who heard his English teacher say repeatedly that one should use the comparative degree when only two things are involved and the superlative when three or more are involved would have to conclude that *best foot forward* must refer to a dog, an octopus or a centipede. But no; it refers to a human being all right. And, as an ancient idiom, it is indeed all right. If you were to say, "Put your better foot forward," friends would start looking around for commitment papers.

BINOCULARS

Since a binocular is a set of two small telescopes, those who speak strictly refer to the instrument as *a binocular*. The rest of us are likely to call the instrument *binoculars* or even *a pair of binoculars*, which, interpreted rigidly, would mean four telescopes. These looser terms are in reputable use and common use, so much so that he who insists on *a binocular* is liable to be regarded as prissy. He is probably the same person who would insist—in these instances erroneously—on "a plier" or "a scissor." *See* PAIR OF TWINS.

BRING

It is, of course, true that when *bring* denotes physical movement, the movement is in the direction of the speaker or writer. But *bring* also has derived uses or figurative uses, and in these senses it is idle to try to make a distinction of physical direction. Thus, you would not say, "Let's try to take him to his senses," nor would you say, "That is a result I would like to take about," nor, if the young actress was successful in her stage appearance, would you say, "She took it off." The verb *come* behaves similarly: When it denotes physical movement, the movement is in the direction of the speaker, but in other senses that is not necessarily true. Thus, referring to a promising young man you don't say, "He is up and going." In short, don't stretch literalness beyond literal functions.

CAN HELP

This is an idiom in reverse English. The words seem to mean the precise opposite of what they are intended to mean and are taken to mean. If you say, "I won't pay more than I can help," you mean "more than I must," or, in straight, unidiomatic words, "more than I cannot help." But the idiom is established and the meaning is never unclear.

CANNOT HELP (BUT)

The fact that *help* has some apparently unrelated meanings (not only to assist but also to be able to prevent or change, as well as to avoid), plus the fact that *but* sometimes has the meaning of only and sometimes of except, produces a series of puzzling idioms. Let us ring the changes on a single (not quite correct) sentence: "Although it is true that our law enforcement authorities should rightly be concerned about militant factions within the ghetto areas, it still remains that brutal attempts to execute a 'final solution' to the problem cannot help fan the fires of hate." Four variations of idiom are possible:

Pompous: ". . . *can but fan the fires of hate*."
Formal: ". . . *cannot but fan the fires of hate*."
Standard: ". . . *cannot help fanning the fires of hate*."
Almost standard: ". . . *cannot help but fan the fires of hate*."

Oddly enough, the only form that is not idiomatic is the one used by the writer of the original sentence. No doubt he was frightened in school by objections he heard to the phrasing "cannot help but." However, he should have disregarded them because they are no longer valid, if they ever were.

CAN'T SEEM

If you say, "He *can't seem* to do his job," you are not, in a literal sense, speaking your mind correctly. It is not the seeming that you intend to negative, but rather the doing of the job. What you mean is, "He seems unable to do his job." Nevertheless, in the *can't seem* construction you are not phrasing your thought incorrectly; you are phrasing it idiomatically.

CLIMB DOWN

Although *climb* has the essential meaning of ascent, *climb down* is in reputable use in its literal sense, as in "He *climbed down* the ladder," and in good informal use in its figurative sense of retreat, as in "The Senator was forced to *climb down* from his lofty oratorical position." The self-contradictory idiom is useful in conveying the suggestion of a more active effort than *descend* or *come down*, which the sticklers would have us use.

COME   *See* BRING.

COULD CARE LESS

The standard idiom, or perhaps smart retort, is, of course, "I couldn't care less." But many conversationalists these days either because their hearing is defective or because they are in an inordinate hurry, or merely because they think it cute, shorten it to "I could care less." Here are the words of an editor, writing to a journalism publication: "Graduates since the U. of W. journalism school went to theory and research could care less about achieving objectivity of any degree in newswriting." At the moment the senseless abbreviated form has not really taken hold, but at the next moment it may, who knows? If it does, it will join "more than I can help" (*see* CAN HELP) as a piece of apparently reverse English.

DO HAVE

Despite some overt opposition, the use of *do* as an auxiliary to *have* has advanced steadily in America, so that it is quite commonplace to hear the question, "*Do* you *have* the time?" and the response, "No, I *don't*." Although the more orthodox speakers and writers in this country tend to avoid the *do* construction, as it is still pretty generally avoided in Britain except as an indication of habit or general tendency, the idiom has found an indisputable place. Sometimes the *do* appears in a response even when it was not suggested in the question: "Have you a good book I may borrow?" "Yes, I *do*." This usage is not quite as acceptable as the other.

DONE

In the sense of completed or finished, *done* split the usage panel of the American Heritage Dictionary almost evenly; 53 per cent found the following sentence acceptable: "The entire project will not be *done* until next year." Webster II labels the usage colloquial; Webster's New World, the Random House and the OED see nothing wrong with it. Who shall decide when doctors disagree? A decade or so hence *done* meaning finished will probably be acceptable to everyone; meanwhile the careful writer will be cautious.

EVERYBODY ELSE'S

Unbelievable as it may sound, there are teachers and

other authorities on English who would have us say, "My hat was on the floor, but everybody's else hat was on the shelf." Says Bryant: "Group genitives that are now well established are *someone else's, nobody else's, everybody else's*, etc., despite the fact that (S.A.) Leonard found in the preparation of *Current English Usage* that the teachers he consulted placed the artificial *everybody's else* among 'established' usages. They must have been influenced by handbooks which were still under the influence of the authoritarian, for the expressions with the *'s* added to *else* are now idiomatic. The linguists, on the other hand, considered *everybody's else* as 'illiterate or semiliterate.' " In one instance either of the two forms is idiomatic: If someone asks, "Is that your wife?" one may say "Who else's wife do you think it is?" or "Whose else do you think it is?" but it should be noted that in the latter instance the possessive form of the pronoun is proper provided the following noun is omitted.

EVERY NOW AND THEN

Bierce not only quarreled with the phrase *now and then*, calling it nonsense because "there can be no such thing as a now and then," but also branded *every* in this context a corruption of *ever*. The phrase may be nonsense, but if so it is ancient nonsense. Even greater nonsense is to try to put the adverb *ever* in front of it. *Now and then* by itself means occasionally. In the phrase at issue the words mean repeated occasions, which demand qualification by an adjective—*every*—not an adverb—*ever*.

FEW, MANY

Both these words present eccentricities that show the power of idiom over logic and grammar. *Few* as a noun is clearly plural. Yet we sometimes put a singular indefinite article in front of it—*a few*—which would lead one to believe it was after all singular. But no; we then place a plural verb after it: "A *few were* chosen for the honors list." Odd, is it not? *Many* is a similar word. Strangely you cannot say *a many*, but you can say *a great many*—and again you follow it with a plural verb: "A *great many were* chosen for the honors list." On the other hand, *many* often figures in an inverted phrase such as many a man, and then—behold—it takes a singular verb: "*Many a man wishes* he had met Helen of Troy." The word also takes a singular verb in the phrase "*Many is* the time." That's idiom for you. See also NUMBER in *Syntax Scarecrows*.

FILL IN (OUT)

Do you *fill in* an application or *fill it out?* Either is good idiomatic English. You may be thinking either of the blanks that require *filling in* or of the entire application that requires *filling out,* i.e., completion. Next question: Is a bottle half full or half empty?

HAND IN HAND

The meaning of this expression is perfectly clear because of the picture it conjures up. Yet you will occasionally see it improperly converted into *hand and hand,* as in this sentence from a news article: "She and Manson walked *hand and hand* along the shore." Ridiculous, you might say; that conjures up no picture at all. Strangely enough, however, *hand and glove,* which likewise does not seem to conjure up much of a picture, is an acceptable alternative to *hand in glove,* whereas *hand and hand* has no standing whatever. (*See also* STILL AND ALL.)

HARD PUT

Although *hard put to it* is the form Follett insists on,

hard put is equally good as an idiom. One meaning of *put* is pushed, thrust or pressed. Therefore, "He was *hard put* to find an explanation" simply means he was hard pressed to find it.

HEAD OVER HEELS

Obviously in normal posture the head is indeed over the heels. Therefore, say the trouble-trackers, the usual expression makes no sense and the phrase should be *heels over head*. Oddly enough, so recent an authority as Webster II accepts *heels over head* as the standard idiom and *head over heels* as a variant. The truth is that *heels over head* was standard in Middle English and the other version was a popular corruption, but so popular that it became standard in the mid-eighteenth century. Today we properly use *head over heels* to describe either a somersaulting plight or an intense state, as in *head over heels* in love or in debt.

I DON'T THINK

Evans in CW says that thousands have written to him to insist that one cannot say "I don't think it's true," because if one says "I don't think" he cannot go on to state the thought he had admittedly not thought. The flaw in this reasoning, as he points out, is the assumption that an adverb (in this instance the *not* that is merged into *don't*) modifies in all instances the word immediately after it. Not infrequently an adverb is what is called a sentence adverb, modifying the entire statement rather than merely the following word. If you say, "I never rode a horse," you are not drawing a distinction between riding a horse and eating one; the *never* modifies the entire thought, not simply *rode*. The *I don't think* construction is entirely correct.

IN HALF

The sticklers tell us not to say, "The budget was cut *in half*," but rather *in halves* or *in two*. Webster II lends them some comfort by terming *in half* colloquial. However, the phrase was used a century ago by Dickens and has been used steadily since. No other dictionary finds it in the least objectionable. It will not do to cite other fractions as analogies because *half* seems to go its own way in other contexts, too. We say *half an hour* when we would not say *quarter an hour*; we say *not half bad* where we would not say *not third bad*; we say *let's go halves* where we would not say *let's go fifths*. In short, *in half* is not in any sense wrong, not by half.

IN (ON) A STREET

Ayres says that we live *in* and that things occur *in*, not *on*, a street. Bierce observes that "a street comprises the roadway and the buildings at each side"; therefore, "Say, *in* the street. He lives *in* Broadway." Evans in CW declares that Americans say *on* and the British say *in*. To complicate matters still further, a couple of editors on a large metropolitan newspaper used to insist that you lived *on* an avenue but *in* a street. If truth there be in so complicated and weighty a matter, Evans seems to have hold of it: If you are American, say *on*; if you are British, say *in*. If you are neither, say, "I give up."

IN (ON) LINE

"Stand *in line*," when you stop to examine it, seems to make more sense than "stand *on line*." This is particularly true if you slip the article *a* in ahead of *line*; *on a line* suggests there is a painted line on the ground. The truth is that *in line* is the preferred, more prevalent expression. *On line* seems to be widespread in New York City and the Hudson

Valley, according to Margaret M. Bryant's *Current American Usage*, and undoubtedly it has been surging outward across the country. It cannot be branded incorrect; the worst that can be said about it is that it is a regional idiom.

IN THE CIRCUMSTANCES *See* UNDER THE CIRCUMSTANCES.

LAND ON WATER

In its original meaning, of course, the verb *land* denotes a touching of shore or a coming to rest on land. But, as so often happens, to the greater glory and richness of the language, the word has expanded from its primary meaning to fill a need. What else could be said of a seaplane finishing a trip except perhaps that it *alighted on the water*, which is correct enough but sounds prissy? To insist on confining words to their original meanings regardless of the need to accommodate new situations is to handcuff the language. *See also* CLIMB DOWN.

ME TOO

Your dinner partner says, "I'd like a brandy," and you chime in, "Me too." Grammatically you are wrong, no matter how right you are in ordering brandy. Grammatically you should be using the nominative case so that your elliptical sentence, when filled out, would go, "I too would like a brandy." Obviously you would not say, "Me too would like a brandy." Having conceded all that, however, let us acknowledge that at least in spoken English *me too* is idiomatic and acceptable, whereas *I too* is grammatical but fairly uncommon.

MUCH LESS

A discussion of when to use *much less* and when to use

much more threatens to become pilpulistic. So, however, be it. There is general agreement that when a statement is affirmative not only in its meaning but also in its wording *much more* is the phrase to use. Example: "He can forgive even his enemies, *much more* his friends." There is also general agreement that when a statement is negative in both its meaning and its wording *much less* is used. Example: "He cannot forgive even his friends, *much less* his enemies." But when the meaning is negative and the wording affirmative, watch out for those split hairs. At this point let us turn to Fowler. He gives this example of a sentence in which both elements are negative: "It is not possible to do it under a year, *much less* in six months." He follows up with—and approves—this example of a sentence in which the meaning is negative but the wording is technically affirmative: "It is impossible to do it under a year, *much more* in six months." Then he explains: "What governs the decision is the words required to fill up the ellipsis: 'It is not possible to do it under a year, much ——? (is it possible to do it) in six months'; 'It is impossible to do it under a year, much ——? (is it impossible) to do it in six months.' " It all sounds very logical until we pilpulists get to work. In the "not possible" sentence he fills up the ellipsis with the words "is it possible," but when you come to examine it why should not the missing words be "is it not possible," which is the idea that the first part of the sentence contained? If those were the missing words, then that sentence too should wind up with a *much more*. Obviously, however, the sentence worded that way would sound wrong. And the reason it would sound wrong is that it would not be idiomatic. The truth of the matter is that *much less* is an idiom; it comes naturally, we don't have to figure out what it means because we know, and we don't have to go back and study some other part of the sentence to see whether it fits.

Much more, on the other hand, is not an idiom. It is far less common than *much less* and it is customarily used with an emphasis that indicates intent rather than habit. We know what we are saying when we use *much more*. When we use *much less* we don't give a thought to the actual meaning of the words, any more than we do to equivalent phrases such as "to say nothing of" or "let alone" or "not to mention"— and what, pray, do those phrases mean really? Even Fowler concedes at the end of his discussion that *much less* is so common that it must be classed among what he calls Sturdy Indefensibles. We can go a step further; *much less* is a sturdy defensible.

MUTUAL FRIEND

Mutual connotes reciprocity or interaction between two or more elements. If A admires B and B admires A, they have a mutual admiration society. But if A admires girls and B admires girls, they do not have a *mutual* admiration for girls, they have a *common* admiration for girls. The sense of "shared in common" for the word *mutual* dates to the late sixteenth century but has long since been relegated to the dustbin of incorrect usage. The only exception is the phrase "mutual friend" or "mutual acquaintance," and Dickens had something to do with that. Perhaps a stronger influence was the fact that the alternative to *mutual* would be *common*, and we don't like to think of our friends as being common.

NOT . . . BUT

Another instance in which logic takes a licking at the hands of idiom is in such a sentence as "He did not intend to write but to phone." Purists would say that "did not intend" would carry over to the second part of the sentence, making hash out of the meaning. They would have us say,

"He intended not to write but to phone." That is fine, but so is the illogical idiomatic construction and the purists have no right to dispute it. *See also* ALL . . . NOT *and* I DON'T THINK.

NO USE

Toward the end of "I Got Plenty o' Nuthin' " in the Gershwin operetta *Porgy and Bess*, Porgy shouts, "No use complainin'! " The purists don't shout any protests about that because after all Porgy is an illiterate. But occasionally they do cry out when literates say the same thing, as most of them do. Strictly speaking, it should be, "no use *in* (or *of*) complaining," but the ellipsis of the preposition has been common at least since 1820 and it is presented as standard by the OUD.

PAIR OF TWINS

Without doubt it is redundant and therefore technically incorrect to refer to a *pair of twins*. One or the other of two creatures brought forth at a single birth is *a twin*; the two together are *twins*. (It should be self-evident that the idea of two underlies the word *twin*.) Therefore, to speak of a *pair of twins* is, technically, to refer to four creatures. Notice the injection of the word "technically" twice in the foregoing lines. The reason for that is that in ordinary, forgivable usage *a pair of twins* is the customary phrase. In some situations it is almost necessary. If you were walking down the street and two like-looking creatures approached, you would probably nudge your companion and say, "They are *twins*"; but if you were relating the incident to a companion who had not been present, you would be quite likely to say, "Coming toward me was *a pair of twins*," rather than "Coming toward me were *twins*." Incidentally and not altogether irrelevantly, "a pair of trousers" is never

questioned, although, of course, "trousers" by itself covers
the thought (as well as the legs). But it should be noted
that no idea of two-ness is inherent in that word. *See* BINOC-
ULARS.

PLIERS *See* BINOCULARS.

SCISSORS *See* BINOCULARS.

SELF-ADDRESSED ENVELOPE

People who are looking for trouble have on occasion objected to the phrase *self-addressed envelope* on the ground
that an envelope does not address itself. But, as Follett says,
their position seems dubious. Technically there should be
no more validity to *self-addressed envelope* than there is to
laurel-rester (*see* BABY-SITTER) because each is a compound
that omits a vital preposition: a *laurel-rester* is one who rests
on his laurels and a *self-addressed envelope* is an envelope
addressed *to* oneself. But whereas *laurel-rester* is not often
used and is not established, *self-addressed envelope* is both.

While the subject of "self-" is before the house a caution
might be sounded about "self-confessed" and "self-
avowed." Both are redundancies because confessing and
avowing are done only by self. Therefore it is sufficient and
preferable to speak of a "confessed murderer" or an
"avowed Communist."

SEND NO MONEY

A disturbed correspondent (and "disturbed" is used here
in every sense of the word) wrote to protest the expression
"Send no money" on the ground that no money would be a
very difficult thing to send. He contended that what the ad
writer had in mind and should have said was, "Do not send
money." Perhaps what the correspondent should have

learned was that when it comes to idiomatic English he should see no evil, hear no evil and speak no evil and then, with the Psalmist, he need fear no evil. For similar nit-picking concerning modifiers see CAN'T SEEM and I DON'T THINK.

SHADES

The challenge to such phrases as *"shades* of Noah Webster!" is so typical of the attitude of those who would try to employ logic to correct idiom that it will get more extended treatment here than the humble little phrase itself would seem to deserve. Since the whole shady business seems to trace back to Bierce, it would be well to begin by quoting his entry:

> Shades *for* Shade. *"Shades of Noah! how it rained!"* *"O shades of Caesar!"* A shade is a departed soul, as conceived by the ancients; one to each mortal part is the proper allowance.

There can be no doubt about it: Logically one shade is all a departed soul should have. Nevertheless, there can also be no doubt that few bodies, if anybody, ever spoke the singular form. Idiom calls for the plural, logical or no. Just why this is so is another and far more mysterious matter. The fact is, however, that there is a real tendency in the language, at least in the spoken language, to pluralize some more or less abstract words when used in colloquial formulas. *Shade* is by no means alone in this respect. Consider, for example, "Good Heavens!" "Land sakes!" or "Sakes alive!" Likewise we say someone is in good "spirits" and we try to avoid hurting his "feelings." We say he has "brains" and has the "makings" of an executive and we haven't seen the "likes" of him in a long time, although at the moment he is in dire "straits." By "rights" he should be an executive by now, and the only trouble is that he—let's get vulgar for a moment—has the "hots" for the boss's secretary; he's "nuts" about her. But in time he should be on all "fours" with the boss and perhaps the boss will let "bygones" be "bygones."

In all these instances the plural is either illogical or at least superfluous. But that is the way people talk. And the way people talk often creates idioms, which bow to neither grammar nor logic.

SKID ROAD (ROW)

To designate a street containing saloons, flophouses and brothels frequented by down-and-outers, both forms are in good standing. The term *skid road* came into use in the latter part of the nineteenth century in the West, where it was applied by loggers first to a path along which logs were hauled to a skidway leading to a body of water and then to the disreputable street in town, which in a different sense was just as rough. When Easterners took up the term half a century later, it became *skid row*, a more citified expression. Although both terms are in use today, *skid row* is the more common.

SPIT AND IMAGE

Most often the users of this phrase say it and write it *spittin' image*." Undoubtedly the reason is that it never occurs to them that the noun *spit* can have anything to do with the expression, and, if they think about *spittin'* at all, they think of it as simply a violent modifier like "damned" in "a damned liar." However, one elderly meaning of *spit* is likeness, and it was and is used in phrases such as "the very *spit* of his father." According to Evans, the *and image* was tacked on in America sometime in the nineteenth century. Interestingly, the French have an analogue of the English phrase: *tout craché*. In any event, *spittin' image*, though it is a corruption of *spit and image*, is just as acceptable these days—assuming, that is, that you like either of them.

STILL AND ALL

Still has the meaning of however or nevertheless, but accounting for *and all* in the dialectal phrase is a little difficult. Webster II defines the whole phrase as meaning nevertheless or after all, and perhaps that takes care of it. In what is at the very least a rare rendition of the expression, Bernard Malamud has a character in *The Fixer* say, "*Still in all*, I'm a loyal subject of the Tsar." There will be no attempt to explain that here.

THAN WHOM

At least as far back as William Cobbett, writing in 1836, proceeding through Bierce in the early nineteen-hundreds, and continuing in some quarters to the present day, authoritarians have been outraged by such phrases as "Cromwell, *than whom* no man was better skilled in artifice." "A hundred phrases might be collected from Blackstone, Hume and even Doctors Blair and Johnson," Cobbett wrote. "Yet they are bad grammar." It takes a bold soul indeed to fly in the face of a hundred phrases penned by writers so distinguished. Cobbett should have had his tip-off in his own assertion. So should Bierce, who wrote, "The misuse of *whom* after *than* is almost universal." Yes, *than whom* is bad grammar all right, but its "almost universal" use by reputable writers has raised it in triumph to the status of good idiom and that is all that counts.

TRY AND

In spoken language *try and* has all but displaced *try to*. That could mean, though it does not necessarily mean, that *try and* is on the way to becoming standard in written language, but it has not achieved that status yet. In some locutions it has a slightly different meaning from *try to,* which denotes merely an essaying of something. In *"try and* keep your chin up" it adds a heartening note, in "I will *try and* write you every day" it adds a note of determination, and in the challenging "You just *try and* make me do it" it contributes a note of defiance and is the only possible phraseology. Still, except when such colloquialisms are being reproduced, good literary usage calls for *try to.*

UNDER THE CIRCUMSTANCES
Some editors insist that the only proper phrase is *in the circumstances.* The reasoning seems to be that *circumstance* literally means a standing around, which would seem to confine it to a horizontal plane. Less literally, however, it means that which surrounds, and the condition of surrounding can assuredly be three-dimensional. The OUD finds both phrases correct and draws this distinction: "Mere situation is expressed by *in the circumstances,* action takes place *under the circumstances.*" Thus, in the circumstances those finicky editors do not seem to have much of a case and under the circumstances they had better retreat before they get their heads knocked in.

USE *See* NO USE.

WOMAN, WOMEN (adj.)
A knot of idiomatic confusion is revealed in this sentence: "Allegations that men attendants have sexually abused girl and women patients at the Greystone Park State Hospital, New Jersey's largest mental institution, are under investigation by the state police." When the name of a being is used adjectivally ahead of a plural noun, is it singu-

lar or plural? No doubt the sticklers would like to have a logical rule. But, alas, if there is a rule at all, it is not logical. Offhand one might be tempted to say the adjectival noun should be plural: *"men attendants, women patients.* But hold! Would you say *girls patients, boys patients, children patients, infants patients, grownups patients?* If anything, the rule is the reverse: Use the singular except for *men* and *women.* It's not logical, but it is idiomatic.

Tangentially, a word may be said here about another way in which men and women are troublesome. The singular form is used when members of either sex are being considered collectively or abstractly: *"Woman's place* is in the home," *man's estate.* The plural form is used when they are being considered concretely as individuals: *women's dormitory, men's club.*

WORST

The phrase *if worst comes to worst* must be wrong, say the superpurists; obviously it should be *if worse comes to worst.* And some of them have tried to impose that piece of misguided logic on the idiom. Idiom it has been since the early 1600's. Thomas Middleton wrote, "The worst comes to the worst," in his play *The Phoenix,* and in the early 1700's the Motteux translation of Cervantes's *Don Quixote* contained the phrase, "Let the worst come to the worst." The words, therefore, have rather aged credentials and should be allowed to live in peace.

In a similar reformist mood Ayres insisted that we must say *at the worst,* not *at worst.* He offered no explanation for his insistence and it is not clear what his reasoning was. Not that there is anything wrong with *at the worst,* but neither is there anything wrong with *at worst,* any more than there is with *at best* or *at most* or *at least.*

Then there is the phrase *get the worst of it,* which has from time to time been a target of the reformers, who argue that if only two things are involved it must be *get the worse of it*. Evans says that "only the form *worst* can be used before *of*, regardless of how many things are being talked about. . . . *Worse of* is unidiomatic English, and the fact that only two objects are being compared is irrelevant." By and large he is correct, but it is possible, if not usual, to speak of "the worse of the two choices."

Spooks of Style

DEAR MISS THISTLEBOTTOM:

In this letter I have collected some of the bugaboos concerning writing style that I have noticed from time to time —dicta that, if taken seriously, would do little to improve an author's product. None of them concern outright errors and few of them concern supposed errors. They seem to fall more into the category of preferences, which have been passed along from teacher to pupil, from editor to reporter, and from generation to generation.

A preference of my own may serve to illustrate how such bugaboos arise and to show that they are not universally applicable. I happen to believe that in news writing, addressed to a reader who is trying to absorb a maximum of information in a minimum of time, simplicity and swift comprehensibility are imperative. The best way to achieve this end, I believe, is to restrict each sentence to a single idea, avoiding a complication of clauses whenever possible. I see no merit in unworkable formulas prescribing the maximum number of words to be used in a sentence. I confine the preference to the single-idea prescription. The sentence may thus contain five words or it may run to a hundred words, though overall the sentences will tend to be shorter rather than longer. Now note that I am talking here only about news writing, which should be designed for a certain limited-time situation. For the reader who opens a book in bed for an hour or so of leisurely reading the situation is quite different. The author writing for that reader might justifiably thumb his nose at my suggestion.

Most of the bugaboos I am presenting here have far less rationale behind them than my own. Indeed, some seem to have none. In any case, style has a quicksilver quality about it, not susceptible to rules that try to pin it down. It is a personal thing with accomplished writers and often they can defy the dicta and still emerge triumphant. For the average writer or the apprentice, only a few generalized suggestions are of value—such precepts as: write naturally, write with economy, choose the precise noun and the forceful verb, strive for clarity.

Yrs., etc.

A, AN, THE, AS OPENERS

It may be that the taboo is restricted to certain journalistic quarters, but without question it exists: Do not begin a story with *a, an* or *the*. One textbook says that "such words rob the story of individuality and vitality" (*Modern Journalism,* Carl G. Miller); a second says that "*a, an* and *the* are considered poor words to open the lead; their frequent use robs the writing of individuality and marks the page as generally monotonous" (*High School Journalism,* Harold Spears); and a third says that the three words "make weak beginnings for leads and should be avoided" (*Journalism,* by William Hartmann).

No doubt those readers who look at the first word of each newspaper story and make comparisons would find it monotonous if each one began with *the,* but are there such readers aside from teachers of journalism? Moreover, suppose a third of the stories began with *the,* another third began with *a* and the remaining third began with *an,* would that be montonous? In actual fact, what happens when young journalists are made conscious of this taboo is that they inadvertently produce a different kind of monotony: They all turn to another form, usually the participial opening. Instead of writing the natural sentence, "The Squeedunk Skunks won a seesaw basketball game against the Flickville Fleas by a score of 86 to 85 last night in the Squeedunk Gym," they all write, "Seesawing to a rousing finish, the Squeedunk Skunks defeated, etc."

It is quite true that *a, an* and *the* are not the strongest words in the English language, but it is doubtful whether using them for openers has any real bearing on the strength or weakness of the sentence they introduce. It is equally doubtful whether reputable authors pay any attention to the taboo.

At hand, by no prearrangement, is *The Short Stories of Henry James* (Modern Library). James, it will be conceded, ranks rather high as a stylist. Here is how one of the stories begins: "The train was half an hour late and the drive from the station longer than he had supposed . . ." Another story starts this way: "The poor young man hesitated and procrastinated: it cost him such an effort to broach the subject of terms . . ." Still a third story has this opening: "The April day was soft and bright, and poor Dencombe . . ." No superstition about the word *the* grips Mr. James, obviously.

When the textbook writers say with what seems to be almost a single voice that beginning a story with one of the three weak articles robs the story of individuality they seem to be laying far too much emphasis on a minor matter. The strength of an opening sentence is determined not by its first word but rather by what it says and how interestingly or forcefully it says it. And as to monotony, that becomes evident only when it calls attention to itself—if, for example, every sentence in the story begins with *the* or if every sentence follows the same structural pattern. In short, the taboo on those first words is by no means the last word.

ADJECTIVES, PLACEMENT OF

Some trouble-trackers are quite insistent on what they believe is the only proper place for the adjective in certain commonplace expressions. They object to "a fine dish of spaghetti," saying it must be "a dish of fine spaghetti"; they get quite heated over "a cold glass of beer" and demand "a glass of cold beer." Their attitude is nothing new. Ayres in 1882 warned against such constructions as, "He has a new suit of clothes and a new pair of gloves," saying, "It is not the suit and the pair that are new, but the clothes and the gloves." Such a dictum may have been (and just possibly may not have been) *de rigueur* in Mr. Ayres's day, but it is *démodé* today. The only rule for constructions of this kind is that they must instantly convey the desired meaning. To be sure, "a plate of large clams" is something different from "a large plate of clams" and "a fine school of the arts" is something different from "a school of the fine arts." But it is rare that the positioning of adjectives causes any confusion.

ALSO

Legitimate objection is made by authorities on usage to starting a sentence with *also* used as a conjunction: "He wore blue jeans and a sweater. *Also* he had a beard." The objection is legitimate because the feeling is inescapable that the writer did not take the trouble to organize what he wanted to say; either he had an afterthought that should have been woven into the first sentence or, if separate emphasis was desired, the second sentence should have been constructed so as to make that clear: perhaps, "To complete the picture, he had a beard." The basic point is that in good usage *also* is used as an adverb, not as a conjunction. That does not mean that no sentence may begin with *also*. When the *also* modifies another word in the sentence it may properly be the first word: "The American flag was in the center. Also conspicuously placed were the British and French flags."

BEST FIVE vs. FIVE BEST

The advice given in Webster II is that superlatives precede numerals used in a collective sense ("The best five examples of architecture," where the thought is of a group of five that is best) and follow those used distributively ("The five best novels of the year," where the thought is not of a group but of five individual novels). That distinction is sometimes difficult to resolve, and most reputable writers have decided that in all such situations "the five best" is good usage.

A few nit-pickers try to make an even finer distinction by arguing that of all novels only one can be best, not five. What they overlook is that a superlative does not necessarily apply to only a single thing; we commonly speak of "the best novels of the nineteenth century," for example. Nit-pickers are sometimes troublemakers.

CLICHÉS

A few years ago, after an operation, my doctor told me I must forgo liquor. When I looked at him in dismay he smiled and said, "If you feel you must have a drink, order a martini with an olive, then take out the olive, shake it well and lick it." I told him I was contemplating no such life as that and he relented. "Well, have just one cocktail a day," he said, "but put water in it." I started ordering martinis and watering them and, lo, I began to find I actually liked them that way. Soon I was telling my friends about my new discovery and each time found myself saying, to fend off their mockery, that I didn't want to sound like the fox that lost its tail, but . . .

For all I know, the licking-the-olive business may be a physicians' cliché, but I had never heard it before. What is certainly a cliché is the fox-that-lost-its-tail phrase, and that was the target of the foregoing elaborate build-up. That phrase is an example of a cliché that is serviceable and not to be scorned. Think of the circumlocution, or perhaps the retelling of the fable, that would be necessary to deliver that fairly simple point if the cliché expression were not at hand. There are others of that variety: *sour grapes, pull the chestnuts out of the fire, teach one's grandmother to suck eggs.* To try to write around such clichés would often lead to pompous obscurity. It is idle to advise a writer, as some authorities do, to avoid clichés. You can't even avoid them in talking about them. The word *cliché* itself, from a French word meaning stereotype, is a cliché. If you define *cliché* as a *stereotype*, you are using a cliché. If you call it a *bromide*, again you are using a cliché. Is it, then, a *hackneyed* expression? *Hackneyed* is a cliché. To get away from clichés you might suggest *new coinages* or *fresh-minted phrases*—in both instances you have run afoul of clichés.

It is not always advisable to get away from clichés by resorting to unaccustomed phraseology. "What is new is not necessarily better than what is old," says Fowler, who then goes on to quote J. A. Spender: "The hardest worked cliché is better than the phrase that fails. . . . Journalese results from the efforts of the nonliterary mind to discover alternatives for the obvious where none are necessary, and it is best avoided by the frank acceptance of even a hard-worn phrase when it expresses what you want to say." What are to be shunned are the well-worn phrases that trickle from the typewriter almost automatically: *in this connection, pick and choose, few and far between, stood him in good stead, wear and tear, as a matter of fact, last but not least.*

If the writer is going to use a cliché it should be evident to the reader that he knows what he is doing. In most instances, for example, the very appropriateness of *on the other hand* will require no apology for its use. Sometimes a sophisticated manner of delivering the cliché—a manner that almost seems to put quotation marks around it—will be effective: "The delegates to the conference seem unable to see the disarmament forest for the weapons trees."

The general caution is not to avoid the use of clichés but rather to use them attentively when they are helpful.

CONNECTIVE WORDS BEGINNING SENTENCES

Eight connective words are involved in the stylistic problem of whether they are suitable to begin sentences: *and, but, for, however, nevertheless, nor, still* and *yet.*

And—The injunction not to begin a sentence with *and* is branded by Follett a "prejudice" and a "false rule." To that, one can only add "Amen" and "Hallelujah." Surely fault cannot be found with the following example in which *and* begins not only a sentence but also a paragraph:

> *Ralph Nader, the consumer lawyer, suggested that consumers were being endangered by a "gaseous verbal balloon floating over the heads of do-nothing Senators."*
> And *Mrs. Bess Myerson Grant, the city's Commissioner of Consumer Affairs, warned of "the danger that we will be fooled by fake reform."*

Fowler, noting that the objection to starting a sentence with *and* is "a faintly lingering superstition," points out that "The OED gives examples ranging from the 10th to the 19th c.; the Bible is full of them." The only warning that is valid is that the device of starting with *and* should not be employed so often that it either becomes noticeable or becomes an affectation.

But—Everything that has been said about *and* applies equally to *but,* though the defense of *but* as a sentence opener is less necessary because the prejudice against this word in that position has greatly diminished.

However—For some reason the feeling against *however* as an opener is strong and persistent, but it is not reasonable. The test for the proper placement of the word is a fairly simple one: It should be so positioned that it throws contrasting emphasis on what precedes it. The following passage from a news story contains two *howevers*, each of which is in the right place even though, be it noted, one of them begins a sentence and a paragraph:

> *That posture has become traditional for mayors of New York in the annual bargaining over the amount of local aid in the state budget. In this election year, however, the bargaining has picked up a new wrinkle in the form of an alliance among the mayors of the "Big Six" cities of the state.*
>
> *Mayor Lindsay's statement before the hearing was to have been read by Mayor Lee Alexander of Syracuse. . . .*
>
> *However, Mayor Alexander was unable to make the trip to Albany because of the weather, so. . . .*

Note that the first *however* puts "this election year" into the desired contrast with what has been "traditional." The second *however* establishes a proper contrast between what had been intended and what actually happened.

Nothing need be said about *for, nevertheless, nor, still* and *yet* as sentence starters because no one has thought (yet?) of raising a taboo against any of them. The fact that such taboos do not exist should in itself suggest how idle are the ones conjured up against almost parallel words.

CONTRACTIONS

Hairsplitters attempt to draw distinctions in contractions, presumably in the interest of precision. Some of them insist that *I'd* always means "I would" and never "I had"; others (or perhaps the same ones) insist that *he's* means

"he is" and not "he has"; still others insist that *I'll* stands
for "I will" and not for "I shall." What the hairsplitters
overlook is that the very act of employing a contraction indicates that the user is putting aside, for the moment at least,
considerations of exactitude in the interest of shortcutting.
The only tests for contractions, therefore, are whether they
are understandable and whether they are in common use.
Those tests ought to rule out the uncommon *it'd*, as in "*It'd*
be too bad if he failed the examination," or "the *President'll*," as in "The *President'll* be disappointed if the bill
fails." And as for the "shall" and "will" distinction, it need
receive no more attention in contractions than in the use of
the words themselves. (*See* SHALL AND WILL.)

Having said all that, one need not go along with Rudolf
Flesch when he says in *The ABC of Style*, "It's a good style
rule to use as many apostrophes as possible . . . the more
contractions you use, the more your writing will resemble
idiomatic, spoken English." (He probably meant, "the
more your writing'll resemble, etc.") One may well challenge the premise that the goal in writing is to duplicate
speaking. Written language and spoken language are different things; obviously writing is and should be the more dis-
ciplined and the more precise.

FRAGMENTARY SENTENCES

For all practical purposes we may define a sentence as a
series of words containing a subject and a predicate. The
inexperienced writer, however, sometimes omits one of
these essentials and the result is what his instructor brands
a fragmentary sentence or a sentence fragment. He will
write, "The man walked down West End Avenue. Where
his home was." Clearly those last four words are not a sentence and should be joined to the first group. The instructor
is right in scribbling "frag" in the margin. Experienced writ-

ers, however, often use fragmentary sentences for rhetorical effect. The difference is that such writers know what they are doing, they do it deliberately rather than accidentally and they do not mislead the reader into expecting a complete sentence. Here are a few examples of acceptable fragments: "The party was as joyous as the occasion it was celebrating. Congenial company, good talk and lilting laughter." "Did the President crush all criticism? By no means." "And what now? Nothing but more talk, more waste and more senseless fighting." Definitely there is a place for fragmentary sentences, but they must be used purposefully: to break the monotony of a series of similar constructions, to vary sentence lengths, to introduce emphasis or to mimic spoken language. But, as is true of any other writing device, they must not be overused, they must not become a mannerism.

INFINITIVE OF PURPOSE

If we write, "He went to the store to buy some bread," no question arises concerning whether he actually made the purchase; the sentence states merely what his intention was. In that context *to buy* is called an infinitive of purpose. On the other hand, if we write, "Smith struck out to end the game," it is perfectly clear that, unless a new Black Sox scandal is brewing, the infinitive does not express Smith's purpose; it states what happened. In between these poles, however, the infinitives can sometimes give rise to ambiguity, as in the following sentence: "Israeli jet planes crossed the Suez Canal today to knock out Egyptian artillery positions on the west bank." Did they do it or was that merely their purpose? Because such an ambiguity can arise, there are those who would use infinitives of that type for expressions of purpose and for nothing else. That is a rather radical therapy. In most instances common sense or the context will make clear what the infinitive means. If the sentence says, "He returned to the house to find his wife had gone out," common sense tells us that he found she had gone out rather than that he returned with the intention of finding she had gone out. If the account says, "Firemen were called to put out the fire," the context will usually inform us that they were successful. If it does not, the fault lies not with the infinitive but with an inadequacy in the account. In general, what is called for is not a narrow restriction on the use of infinitives but rather care to make sure there is no doubt or misunderstanding.

INVERTED WORD ORDER

Normally in English the subject precedes the verb, but there are exceptions, such as the interrogatory sentence ("Are you leaving?"), the exclamatory sentence ("Zing went the strings of my heart") and the hypothetical sentence ("Had they but known, they might have escaped"). What arouse some authoritarians are a few other variations that writers occasionally indulge in as an affectation. The writer who thinks he is boring the reader by repeating "he said" too often may serve up a sentence like this: " 'I'm quite a comedian,' chuckled he." Or the news magazine that sets great store by idiosyncratic style may offer us, "Sighed a weary federal mediator after negotiations had stalled: 'One side is talking Chinese and the other French.' " But justifiable condemnation of such mannerisms should not lead to condemnation of all sentence inversions. In newspaper writing, for instance, it might be better to say, "Subscribing to the petition were," followed by half a dozen names of organizations and individuals, than to begin with the names and keep the reader in suspense until the verb appears. (That, by the way, is a rare instance; usually such a sentence could begin with *those* and proceed in normal order.) A similar desire to avoid undue delay—and undue subordination of an element that calls for notice— might dictate phrasing a sentence this way: "Into the street jammed with demonstrators swept a phalanx of helmeted police, swinging their clubs and ordering the crowd to disperse." On some occasions a phrase worthy of a prime position will properly throw the sentence into inversion: "Second only to the President is the Secretary of State in the discussions now going on." On other occasions it is desirable to alert the reader early to some element of what is being said: "Only after the House has acted will the Senate be in a position to bring its views to bear on the appropriations bill that has caused so much debate." Sentence inversion is bad only perhaps, not per se.

IT *See* THERE, BEGINNING A SENTENCE.

LATE, THE

Do you use *the late* for anyone at all who has crossed the River Styx? Obviously not, for you would not speak of *"the late* Julius Caesar." Likewise you would not normally expect to see someone who died only yesterday referred to in that manner. Still there is at least one newspaper that does it; if a child was accidentally killed in a shooting affray yesterday, the caption of today's news picture will inevitably read *"The late* Amanda Krum." One usage is almost as ridiculous as the other. What, then, is the rule? Alas, there is none, except perhaps to rule out the two extremes just cited. If the person is someone who was prominent, probably *the late* is so superfluous that it should not be used: Winston Churchill, President Kennedy, Marcel Proust, for example. If it is someone who was not prominent, the statute of limitations might run for half a century. But for someone who has just died, perhaps the body should be allowed to

cool for a month or so before the adjective is applied and in
the meanwhile the phrase "who died on July 15" might be
used.

One caution may be sounded here. Although some dictionaries define *late* as meaning recently gone out of office,
it is best not to apply the word in this sense to an individual. It is quite acceptable to speak of "the *late* Administration," but it would be ambiguous to speak of "the *late* President."

See also THEN.

LIKE, SUCH AS

The difference between these two means of comparison is
slight. *Such as* seems to invite the reader into a category of
comparable things; *like* makes a more direct comparison.
Yet some nit-pickers object to saying, "German composers
like Beethoven," arguing that no composers were like Beethoven and that we should say *such as*. The argument is
specious because *like* does not necessarily mean identical.

MARRIED

James Gordon Bennett the younger, as editor of *The
New York Herald,* insisted that a man *marries* a woman, a
woman *is married* to a man. His insistence on this point has
carried over to society pages of this day. He may have been
harking back to the sentiment expressed by Ayres: "Inasmuch as the woman loses her name in that of the man to
whom she is wedded, and becomes a member of his family,
not he of hers—inasmuch as, with few exceptions, it is her
life that is merged in his—it would seem that, properly,
Sally Brown is married to John Jones. . . ." O tempora, o
mores; tempus fugit, and perhaps sic transit gloria mundi.
A second consideration in Mr. Bennett's thinking may have
had something to do with the etymological origin of the

word *marry*, which is related to the Latin *maritus*, meaning husband. Whatever the consideration, it was misguided. Dictionaries are unanimous in saying that either sex can do it to the other.

A quite separate question concerns the phrase *got married*. Ayres terms this one a vulgarism and Bierce says: "If this is correct we should say, also, 'got dead' for died; one expression is as good as the other." Without question, *got married* is gauche. Still, there are occasions when it is necessary. If you say, "She was married in 1965," it may not be clear whether you are referring to a ceremony or to the resulting state. Or, to take Curme's example, you might have a sentence like this: "He is married now, but I can't tell you when he got married." The occasions for the constructions may be rare, but they suggest that a rigid ban is inadvisable.

MEANTIME

The American Heritage Dictionary carries this usage note: "*Meantime* serves principally as a noun: 'In the *meantime*, we waited.' In expressing the same sense by a single adverb, *meanwhile* is more common than *meantime*: '*Meanwhile*, we waited.'" If this note was intended as a caution, it may safely be disregarded. *Meantime* as an adverb has an ancient history. The American Heritage itself cites a sentence from Shakespeare the Avon Bard, who in this respect was not avant-garde: "Meantime, let wonder seem familiar." Moreover, Bartlett's classic *Concordance of Shakespeare* lists no fewer than sixteen similar uses of *meantime* and a mere four such uses of *meanwhile*.

MIXAPHORS

The mixaphor, known as the mixed metaphor heretaphor, is too well known to require extensive illustration. Some specimens are of the obvious, ludicrous variety: "The internal strife gnawing at the country has not only mirrored the 'cold war' but also brought it to a hot focus from time to time." Other specimens are perhaps less obvious but just about as ludicrous: "The ecologists are hammering away at the population growth bottleneck in an effort to shave it to reasonable proportions." What is less well known is the difference between the mixed metaphor and successive metaphors. If a poet writes, "My lass is a lovely flower, she is the silver moon on a springtime night," he is not mixing metaphors; he is piling them up. Or if a reporter writes, "The war issue itself is water over the dam now, and many Senators hope it will be all but forgotten; but before the elections in the fall a major effort will be required to mend the wounds inflicted in the debate," he is not mixing metaphors but rather switching from one to another. As Follett puts it, "It is not the mere succession of incompatible images that offends reason, but the joining of these images into, as it were, a working piece of machinery."

MONOLOGOPHOBIA

Definition: An overwhelming fear of using a word more than once in a single sentence, or even in a single paragraph. *Etiology*: As a child the patient probably was compelled to stand in a corner because he wrote, in a composition: "Grandma gave me a piece of apple pie, then I had another piece of apple pie and then I had another piece of apple pie." *Symptoms*: The patient now writes: "The wife gave me a piece of apple pie, then I obtained another slice of the pastry containing the round, fleshy fruit, and then I secured another portion of the all-American dessert." As is evident, monologophobia is usually accompanied by violent synonymomania. *Treatment*: Gently suggest to the patient that repetition is not necessarily fatal, but that if it is an intrusive manifestation, the corrective is not a conspicuous synonym but rather an inconspicuous pronoun or noun: "another," "a second," "a third one."

Monologophobia, accompanied by synonymomania, is an ailment to which sports writers are sometimes susceptible. A few of them are prone to write: "The home team scored one run in the first inning, two in the third frame and three more in the seventh stanza." There are legitimate variables in that sentence—the runs scored in each inning; why confuse things by making what should be a constant look like a variable? Why make the reader wonder, if only momentarily, whether innings, frames and stanzas are different things?

Repetition that is conspicuous is, of course, undesirable. A touch of synonymomania would not hurt a sentence like this: "United States help is expected to be helpful over the years in helping the African country to get on its feet." But sometimes repetition is deliberate and forceful: "God helps them that help themselves." What is not desirable is the practice that Fowler terms "elegant variation": calling a cat a "slinky feline" or calling gold "the precious yellow metal."

NOUNS AND VERBS vs. MODIFIERS

Two schools of thought compete for the favor of the apprentice trying to make his writing style effective. One is the Modifier School and the other is the Noun-Verb School. Let a spokesman for each set forth his case. First, hear the Modifier man:

> . . . *What you wish to say is found not in the noun but in what you add to qualify the noun. The noun is only a grappling iron to hitch your mind to the reader's. The noun by itself adds nothing to the reader's information; it is the name of something he knows al-*

*ready, and if he does not know it, you cannot do busi-
ness with him. The noun, the verb and the main clause
serve merely as a base on which the meaning will rise.
The modifier is the essential part of any sentence.* *

Now hear the Noun-Verb man:

*Write with nouns and verbs, not with adjectives and
adverbs. The adjective hasn't been built that can pull
a weak or inaccurate noun out of a tight place. This is
not to disparage adjectives and adverbs; they are indispensable parts of speech. . . . In general, however, it
is nouns and verbs, not their assistants, that give to
good writing its toughness and color.*†

As is true of all advocates, neither is quite as tough as he
sounds. The Noun-Verb man disclaims an attempt to disparage adjectives and adverbs, and the Modifier man manages to write his brief without including a single modifier of
the type he is talking about. Therefore, the one should not
be taken to mean "Never use modifiers" and the other
should not be taken to mean "Always use modifiers." The
question that arises, however, is, Which has the better case?

In the pedagogical electorate there can be little doubt
that the votes go to the Noun-Verb School. "Nouns and
verbs are the guts of the language," says Alan H. Vrooman
in *Good Writing, An Informal Manual of Style.* "If you
pick the right noun or verb, the qualifying adjective or adverb is often unnecessary." In *The Golden Book on Writ-*

---

* John Erskine, "A Note on the Writer's Craft," *Twentieth Century
English*, New York, 1946.
† E. B. White, "An Approach to Style," in *The Elements of Style*, by
William Strunk Jr. and E. B. White, New York, The Macmillan Company,
1959.

ing, by David Lambuth and others, this passage appears: "Nouns and verbs are the bones and sinews of speech. Nouns build up the bony structure of the sentence, verbs produce motion. The more concrete nouns and active verbs you use, the more forceful your writing. The novice naturally imagines that piling up adjectives adds definiteness and that sticking in adverbs adds intensity, but it is usually just the other way round. Adjectives and adverbs are often necessary to complete your meaning and make it exact, but they lessen the force of the sentence unless you dole them out stingily as a miser doles out gold." Sir Ernest Gowers in *The Complete Plain Words* (Pelican Books) declares: "It has been wisely said that the adjective is the enemy of the noun" [Voltaire, by the way, is supposed to have been the wise man] and proceeds, "Cultivate the habit of reserving adjectives and adverbs to make your meaning more precise, and suspect those that you find yourself using to make it more emphatic. Use adjectives to denote kind rather than degree."

Nevertheless, many good writers lean heavily on modifiers but, because they are good writers, select the modifiers carefully. This practice is illustrated in the following passage from Katherine Anne Porter's *Ship of Fools:* "Ric and Rac, Lola's twins, got up early and dressed themselves quietly before Lola and Tito were awake. They were badly buttoned and frowsy-haired; their wary black eyes gave their sallow sharp faces a hardened, precociously experienced look; awake, they were up to mischief, and asleep, they dreamed of it."

On the other hand, Vladimir Nabokov, an outstanding modern stylist, uses scarcely any modifiers in the following opening passage from *Speak Memory*, yet achieves undeniable power: "The cradle rocks above an abyss, and common sense tells us that our existence is but a brief crack of light between two eternities of darkness. Although the two are identical twins, man, as a rule, views the prenatal abyss with more calm than the one he is heading for (at some forty-five hundred heartbeats an hour)." Similarly barren of modifiers, yet beautiful, is the Twenty-third Psalm:

> *The Lord is my shepherd; I shall not want;*
> *He maketh me to lie down in green pastures:*
> *He leadeth me beside the still waters. He*
> *   restoreth my soul:*
> *He leadeth me in the paths of righteousness*
> *   for his name's sake.*
> *Yea, though I walk through the valley of the*
> *   shadow of death,*
> *I will fear no evil: for Thou art with me;*
> *Thy rod and Thy staff they comfort me.*
> *Thou preparest a table before me in the*
> *   presence of mine enemies:*
> *Thou anointest my head with oil; my cup*
> *   runneth over.*
> *Surely goodness and mercy shall follow me all*
> *   the days of my life:*
> *And I will dwell in the house of the Lord*
> *   for ever.*

How, then, shall we adjudicate between the Noun-Verb School and the Modifier School? The decision will have to lean toward the Noun-Verb advocates. That is by no means to say that adjectives and adverbs are to be banished; we cannot do without them. But concentration on the nouns and the verbs will lead to less looseness of expression and to a greater likelihood of precision. The writer will not be content with a generalized, perhaps abstract, word that he thinks he can sharpen with a modifier. He will seek out the strong, exact word that needs no modifier. To take an absurdly simple example, he might without thought set down:

He looked up intently at the clear, blue sky above.

Patently *up* and *above* are redundant adverbs and *clear* and *blue* are redundant adjectives except that the second one tells us it is not nighttime. In addition, a little thought will suggest that a single word can express more sharply the thought of *looked intently*. Such attention to the selection of words with just the desired meaning might produce a more compact, more forceful sentence:

He gazed at the bright sky.
or
He peered at the bright sky.

For the novice at least, attention should be focused on nouns and verbs. That way lies strength in writing.

ONE
After you have begun using *one* in a sentence, what word do you use to refer to it later on? What is required, ideally, is a singular pronoun of common gender, since *one* is singular and has no gender. But, alas, English lacks such a pronoun. In Elizabethan days the solution was to use *he*. Thus, you will find in Shakespeare, "I know the more one sickens, the worse at ease he is." But the British later on turned their backs on this usage and began to insist on repeating *one*, no matter how nauseating the repetition became. Take a look at these lines from Browning: "Alack! one lies oneself / Even in the stating that one's end was truth, / Truth only, if one states so much in words." To this day the Brit-

ish still cling to *one*, regardless of how many times it comes
up in a sentence. In this country the authorities followed
the British lead right through the nineteenth century, insisting that *one* was the only reference word, though occasionally suggesting that the way out of the trap was to use *a
man* or *we* in the first instance. Today, however, we have
parted company with the British and the preference here is
to use *he* in subsequent references. In addition, we often
shun the *one* in the first place and substitute the genderless,
common-number *you*. *See* YOU, THE READER.

ONLY

Trouble-trackers take great delight in pointing out what
they consider misplaced *only*'s. They insist that the word
only must always be placed in direct contact with the element of the sentence that it qualifies. Thus, to borrow an
example from Fowler, they veto "He only died a week ago"
and demand "He died only a week ago." The second version is, without doubt, prissy-pure, but the first is a completely natural way of putting it and contains not the slightest invitation to misunderstanding. It may be conceded that
normally the placing of *only* close to the element it qualifies
is best. But there are at least three exceptions to the "normal" placement that are preferable. One is a situation in
which idiom dictates an "abnormal" placement. For instance: "What is occurring in the African country can only
be called a revolution." The "normal" position for *only*
would be ahead of "a revolution," but that position would
be unnatural and would also suggest a meaning different
from the intended one; it might indicate a minimizing of
the "revolution" idea. A second exception is not really a deviation from normality but seems so; it is a situation in
which the *only* is a sentence adverb qualifying the entire
statement rather than a part of it. For instance: "He only

thought he was being helpful." A third exception is a situation in which the writer wishes to alert the reader early in the sentence to the fact that there is a string attached to the statement. "Normal" positioning would call for a sentence in this form: "The revised welfare bill will pass both the House and the Senate at this session only if liberal Republicans line up with the Democratic majority." But it would be better to give the reader an early warning signal by placing the *only* ahead of *pass*. There is little disagreement among authorities about these exceptions to the normal order, but the trouble-trackers keep their muskets cocked just the same.

ON THE OTHER HAND

Sentries of style sometimes object to the use of *on the other hand* if the first hand has not been mentioned. The objection may be overruled with little ado. Conceivably some reader, encountering *on the other hand* when no manus has been mentioned previously, might pause and say, "What other hand?" If such a reader exists he must be the same fellow who would ask, "What does that writer mean by 'sour grapes'?" A parallel exists there because *on the other hand* is a useful cliché just as *sour grapes* is. The normal reader does not think of a cliché in terms of its literal meaning, but rather grasps its abstract sense. If he reads that his Senator is "sitting on the fence," he realizes at once that the Senator is not taking sides; he does not conjure up a picture of the Senator perched atop a railing. In the same way when he reads *on the other hand* he simply shifts direction and does not give that initial hand a first thought. *See also* CLICHÉS.

PARAGRAPHS

Once before, I wrote that an elementary school teacher

told her class that a paragraph could not contain only one sentence. When an impertinent pupil asked her why, she replied that obviously if it had only one sentence it would be a sentence, not a paragraph. I wrote then and I repeat now: That teacher deserves a sentence—and a long one.

One cannot be arbitrary about paragraphing. It is a means of grouping thoughts, but much more it is a visual device. Much depends on the subject, the typography, the purpose of what is being written, the readers to whom it is addressed and the conditions under which they are likely to read it. A doctoral thesis or a scientific paper may have longer paragraphs than a children's story. In newspapers, where the narrow columns tend to elongate paragraphs and where the reader should be speeded on his way, paragraphs are usually short. In a work intended to be read with great concentration in seclusion and quiet (will somebody turn off that rock music over there?) paragraphs can be longer and customarily are.

A handbook at my elbow has three short sections on this subject. They are headed "Avoid a series of short choppy paragraphs," "Avoid a series of long, heavy paragraphs" and "Make sure that paragraphs are correctly proportioned." Any questions?

PASSIVE VOICE

With a good degree of unanimity, authorities on writing style advise use of the active voice in preference to the passive: "John loves Mary" in preference to "Mary is loved by John." But apprentice writers should not translate this counsel into "Avoid the passive voice." Without doubt the passive often produces a weaker sentence than the active and it usually requires more words. Nevertheless, it is unobjectionable in at least four situations:

1. When the thing done is the significant part of what is

being said and the agent performing the action is too obvious or unimportant to mention: "Smith was arrested in mid-July and indicted a month later in the downtown bombing." "Cloudy, cold weather was forecast for today's parade."

2. When the agent performing the action is indefinite or unknown: "More vandalism is being reported in the city these days than ever before."

3. When the passive voice helps in positioning an element of the sentence at the end for emphasis: "The famous poem about Chicago was written by Carl Sandburg." "We can't use our television set because it is being repaired."

4. When the desire is to convey an air of detachment and to avoid the forceful language that the active voice sometimes produces. This quiet tone is favored particularly in the fields of science and diplomacy: "Patients with severe lacerated or punctured wounds caused by objects soiled with dust, pavement brush burns and wounds or compound fractures should be given much larger amounts of tetanus antitoxin than the customary dose . . . particularly when first given several days after the injury was received." "The United States delegation has been given the impression that the attitude of the other side has been somewhat modified."

When a list like the foregoing is drawn up, there is often a postscript. The postscript in this instance concerns a use of the passive voice that does not deserve to rank with the four others. The passive voice is sometimes desirable to relieve the monotony of a string of similarly constructed sentences using the active voice. But even in such a situation it may be better to achieve variety by altering the structure of a sentence in the midst of the monotony.

POSSESSIVES WITH LONG PHRASES

Exception could hardly be taken to such possessive constructions as "my big brother Joe's home" or "Gilbert and Sullivan's operettas" or "the chairman of the governing board's decision." But when the long phrase produces clumsiness, the 's at the end is best avoided; for example: "She is the man who took care of our baggage's sister" or, even more ridiculous, "Who do you suppose's hat that is?"

PREPOSITION AT END

A friend of mine—let's call him Buster—who is a high school English teacher tells me that a colleague of his encountered him on the way to lunch one day and said, "Here's something you will appreciate. The kids in my history course had to write a short piece on the Civil War and, believe it or not, I spent a quarter of an hour lecturing them on not ending a sentence with a preposition. That's not my subject, but I felt I had to do it because the offenses in their writing were so flagrant." Then, according to Buster, the conversation went something like this:

"I don't know what you're getting at," said Buster, as solemnly as he could.

"I was telling them," said the colleague, "that it wasn't good English to end a sentence with a preposition."

"I still don't know what you are talking about," said Buster.

"Are you kidding?" said the colleague. "You're an English teacher, aren't you? I talked to them about the rule that you shouldn't end a sentence with a preposition. You understand that, don't you?"

"Maybe you don't know what rules are for," said Buster, still with a straight face.

The colleague looked at him for a moment, puzzled and annoyed, then said, "I don't know what you're up to, but . . ."
"You mean you don't know to what I am up," said Buster, "or perhaps up to what I am. Right?"

I am not sure they are on speaking terms any more.

So many authorities on usage have tried to correct the impression that it is wrong to end a sentence with a preposition that I almost feel as if I were flogging a dying horse. But the horse doesn't die. Every now and again some blindfolded rider trots him out on his rickety legs and prods him into whinnying, "Nay." I get the feeling that some pedagogues have been feeding him on the sly—perhaps in the open.

The origin of the misguided rule is not hard to ascertain. To begin with, there is the meaning of the word "preposition" itself: stand before. The meaning derives from Latin, and in the Latin language prepositions do usually stand before the words they govern. But Latin is not English. In English prepositions have been used as terminal words in a sentence since the days of Chaucer, and in that position they are completely idiomatic.

It is true that sometimes a preposition at the end causes the sentence to die with a whimper. Here is an instance: "Cheltenham is not a good type to set the body of a book in." It must be remembered that the end of a sentence is a conspicuous position and can be one of strength. To fill it in the foregoing illustration with that shy little word *in* is to surrender a position of strength. That is not true, however, in such idiomatic sentences as, "I don't know what you are talking about," or, "You don't know what rules are for." In each of those sentences the stress falls toward the end, and the words are sufficiently strong to sustain that stress. Incidentally, you would find it most difficult to recast those sentences to avoid ending them with prepositions.

What strict-constructionist teachers have been describing as a syntactical deficiency is set down by some authorities as a positive asset. "The fact is," says Fowler, "that the remarkable freedom enjoyed by English in putting its prepositions late and omitting its relatives is an important element in the flexibility of the language." And Curme says: "Thus for many centuries the position of a preposition at or near the end of a proposition has been one of the outstanding features of our language."

PUNS

Puns are the easiest form of humor, but it does not follow that they are the lowest form. Any more than it follows that because it is easy to make coffee no one can make a fine cup of coffee. Charles Lamb said: "A pun is a noble thing per se. O never bring it in as an accessory! . . . it fills the mind; it is as perfect as a sonnet; better" (Letter to Coleridge).

There are some, however, who abominate the pun. Arthur G. Kennedy in *Current English* went so far as to suggest doing something about homonyms, words that sound alike but have different meanings (*grown* and *groan*, for example). "The chief solution of the difficulty resulting from the confusion of homonyms," he wrote, "is still to be found in the very simple expedient of dropping one of the pair from use, and there is no better illustration of this evasive method than the story of the Englishman who enjoyed the humorous explanation of the American fruit-grower that 'we eat what we can and what we can't we can,' but later reported to his friends at home that 'they eat what they can and what they can't they put up in tins.' " If Mr. Kennedy was suggesting deliberate tampering with the language, the campaign was ill-advised, but fortunately it is not likely to get very far.

Puns were at least as prevalent in Elizabethan days as they are today, but there was a difference. The Greenough book points out that "the Elizabethans did not laugh at puns, unless they were peculiarly amusing. They got merely a certain intellectual titillation out of the grotesque association of ideas which punning induced." One passage from Shakespeare's *Comedy of Errors* illustrates both types of word play. Dromio of Syracuse is telling his master Antipholus about the globular woman who claims him, and among the amusing, even low-grade, remarks are these: "I have but lean luck in the match, and yet she is a wondrous fat marriage," and, when asked what is her name, "Nell, sir;—but her name and three-quarters, that is an ell and three-quarters, will not measure her from hip to hip." The quiet intellectual titillation comes a moment later after Dromio says, "She is spherical, like a globe; I could find out countries in her," and Antipholus asks, "In what part of her body stands Ireland?" "Marry, sir, in her buttocks: I found it out by the bogs," Dromio replies. Eric Partridge in *Shakespeare's Bawdy* notes that *by* is used in two senses: beside and by means of; he also speculates that *the bogs* may also have had a double meaning since it at one time was a synonym for a latrine or privy, but other evidence suggests that this meaning may not have taken hold quite that early. At another point Antipholus, pursuing the same line of inquiry, asks, "Where stood Belgia,—the Netherlands?" and Dromio says, "O, sir, I did not look so low," a clear pun on the term Low Countries.

Double meanings provide intellectual, nay sensual, titillation in this passage from Shakespeare's "Venus and Adonis," in which Venus says:

I'll be a park, and thou shalt be my deer;
Feed where thou wilt, on mountain or in dale:
Graze on my lips; and if those hills be dry,
Stray lower, where the pleasant fountains lie.
Within this limit is relief enough,
Sweet bottom-grass, and high delightful plain,
Round rising hillocks, brakes obscure and rough,
To shelter thee from tempest and from rain;
Then be my deer, since I am such a park;
No dog shall rouse thee, tho' a thousand bark.

Not the least of the double meanings there is the word "relief," which is used in the sense of gratification of desire and in the sense of contrasting physical contours.

Lamb, however, was impatient with the esoteric pun. "A pun," he said, "is a pistol let off at the ear; not a feather to tickle the intellect" ("Popular Fallacies"). Plenty of those pistols bark these days. And some of them misfire. Plays on words that are so obvious that a discriminating writer would disdain to touch them and so lacking in a genuine double meaning that they are not even amusing are sure to be duds. One example will suffice. Two young polar bears were introduced to each other at the Central Park Zoo in New York and the headline on the news story said, "Snowball Meets Scandy and is Barely Affected." See?

Today the pistols are firing at us from every direction. Advertisers particularly are constantly taking aim at us. From a single Sunday issue of *The New York Times* here are some of the potshots that retailers fired: Wigs: "Headline excitement." Two-piece knit dress: "A plum of a pair." Bathing suit: "Slink or swim." Clothes: "Traveling companions." Shoes: "Give yourself a lift." Perfumes: "We want you to meet some friends that make scents." Butcher's block and knives: "A cut above the rest." Obviously puns are the easiest form of humor.

But it is not only advertisers who have found merit in the pun; serious writers in recent times—Joyce, Cheever, Nabokov—have put it to effective use. At the turn of the century the Greenough book observed, "Puns are now out of favor," but that statement is no longer true. Naturally, bad puns are out of favor and always will be. But the really good pun—the kind that not only invokes two senses of a word but also makes meaningful use of both senses—will always be esteemed. When an art writer, Grace Glueck, reviewing an exhibition of sketches by Larry Rivers, terms him "one of our top drawers," one can only smile, make a deep bow and murmur, "Your grace."

REASON WHY

It might be well to dispose of *the reason is because* before delving into *the reason why*. The principal objection raised against both of them is that both constructions are redundant. *Because* does indeed mean for the reason that and to say "the reason is because" is indeed a redundancy. The objection to that phraseology is valid enough, particularly since it can always be avoided with a perfectly idiomatic substitute. If a sentence reads "The reason he did not go was because he was ill," it can be changed to either "He did not go because he was ill" or "The reason he did not go was that he was ill." Both versions are idiomatic and preferable. The objection to *the reason why* is on less solid ground. *Why* does in one of its meanings denote the reason for which, but it also can denote on account of which, and if it has the latter meaning no tautology arises when it is used after *reason*. Moreover, it cannot be omitted indiscriminately without sometimes resulting in an unidiomatic locution. Nonscientific study and inexhaustive thought lead to the following three conclusions:

> *Conclusion I—When* reason *stands at the head of a sentence, no* why *is necessary: "The reason he is tired is overwork." This conclusion is qualified by the next momentous conclusion.*
> *Conclusion II—When anything intervenes between* reason *and the clause, a* why *is necessary: "I see no reason, sound or unsound, why he is tired."*
> *Conclusion III—When a negative precedes* reason, *a* why *is necessary: "No reason why he is tired can be found," "There is not a reason on earth why he is tired."*

Examination of a goodly number of samples suggests that the *why* is necessary more often than it is dispensable and it is never unidiomatic, and never wrong.

SHALL AND WILL

Many of us remember how our teachers drilled into us that to express simple futurity we should use *shall* in the first person and *will* in the second and third persons, whereas to express determination we should reverse that order. Yes, we well remember their drilling that into us, but we quickly forgot or neglected to apply that formula. The facts of usage are that the distinction simply is not made and *will* is used in just about all situations. On some occasions *shall* crops up to lend a touch of formality and perhaps determination, but otherwise it is for the most part neglected. Maybe it is so as not to offend our dear teachers, but most of us retreat, in speech at least, behind the contractions—*I'll, he'll, you'll, they'll*—and no one can tell whether we mean *will* or *shall*. But one clue to what we mean lies in the disinclination, in America, at any rate, to use *sha'n't*. We would not for a moment scorn anyone who chose to follow the old school formula, but in return we do not wish to be scorned for ignoring it. *See also* CONTRACTIONS.

SLANG

Time was when the use of slang in respectable writing was as reprehensible as belching aloud at the dinner table. Here is what Ayres said of slang in 1882:

"It is always low, generally coarse and not unfrequently foolish. With the exception of cant, there is nothing that is more to be shunned. We sometimes meet with persons of considerable culture who interlard their talk with slang expressions, but it is safe to assert that they are always persons of coarse natures."

If Ayres felt that strongly about the use of slang in speech, the mind boggles at what he must have thought about its use in the more careful form of communication, writing.

Times have changed, however, and language, along with many other human conventions, has relaxed somewhat. There is little left of what might be called formal language, although we do still find it in court decisions, State of the Union messages, diplomatic correspondence, editorials in staid newspapers, commencement addresses and scientific papers. Even in these we occasionally run across a bit of unbending. A history professor writes in a solemn article that "a little history might be trotted out" and, proceeding to trot it out, tells us that a puppet Vietnamese ruler "failed to pan out." A dignified United States Senator speaks of "this new ball game" in our foreign policy. A Chicago judge, in a racial case, congratulates the state's attorney for taking a step toward "cooling it." An editorial in *The New York*

Times suggests that the President "has lost his cool." A news story in the same journal says that a Georgia town has a reputation for harboring "clip joints" to "fleece" visitors. And, wonder of wonders, a monograph on linguistics, one of the stuffiest items this side of the Thanksgiving turkey, at one point startlingly introduces the word "okay" and at another loosens up with the phrase "all this is old hat." Times have changed indeed.

It would be folly to admonish writers never to use slang. Much depends on the tone desired in the writing. Many novels today deliberately strive for earthiness; they read almost as if they were being spoken rather than written. In such writing slang is quite in place. At the other extreme is the stuffy linguistics monograph, so recondite and turbid that the rare injections of slang jolt the reader by their intrusiveness. Between these extremes lies the relaxed, person-to-person style of most writing today, and there a modicum of slang is tolerable.

Most slang tends to be ephemeral. But there are some terms that last. They are peculiarly necessary, either because the thought cannot be expressed otherwise or because the expression of it would take a cumbersome phrase. In this category are "broke" (lacking in funds), "fix" (a form of collusion), "frame-up," "hijack," "mug" and "mugging" (referring to a particular kind of felonious assault) and "racket." It is safe to predict that most, if not all, of these words, now classed as slang or informal, will find complete acceptability before too long.

As to the faddish, up-to-the-minute slang expressions, they are best avoided in reputable writing, except when they are used with deliberation to convey a tone. If there is doubt about whether to use them or not, lean toward the not.

SUCH AS, LIKE *See* LIKE, SUCH AS.

THE (as in "Motherwell, the painter")

One school of thought, if thought is the right word, contends that you should not write "Motherwell, the painter" because there is more than one painter. The implication in that contention is that the use of *the* indicates there is only one. Dictionaries tell us, however, that the article designates uniqueness or preeminence. Note the alternative. When you speak of "Motherwell, the painter" you are not intending to say, nor are you saying, that he is the only painter; what you are doing is ellipsizing* *famous* or *noted* or some other such word. If you were to come right out and say "Motherwell, the famous painter," no one would accuse you of declaring that he was the only famous painter. So much for that issue. But there are other, tangential issues about the designation of the famous, the near-famous and the scarcely known that often confront writers. These issues are best resolved by thinking of four categories of above-ordinary people: first, those who are so preeminent in their fields that they require no identification at all (Beethoven, Shakespeare, Newton); second, those who are a cut or two lower and are not quite so well-known, and for these a *the* might be appropriate (Glinka, the composer; Uris, the novelist; Watson, the biochemist); third, those who have come into semiprominence, for whom a noun with no article would seem to be proper (Burt Bacharach, composer; John Ciardi, poet; Hideki Yukawa, physicist); and, fourth, those who are struggling and hope to be known, for whom an *a* is all they merit (Jack Glutz, a composer; Evelyn Whozis, a poet; Dr. Erich Weisenheimer, a chemist). Assigning people to one or another of those categories is not

---

* See ELLIPSIZE in the Witchcraft in Words section.

the simplest job in the world, but it is not the most difficult either.

THEN

Referring to such locutions as "the then Governor," Ayres wrote in 1882: "The use of this word as an adjective is condemned in very emphatic terms by some of our grammarians, and yet this use of it has the sanction of such eminent writers as Addison, Johnson, Whately and Sir J. Hawkins. Johnson says, 'In his then situation,' which, if brevity be really the soul of wit, certainly has much more soul in it than 'In the situation he then occupied.' However, it is doubtful whether 'then,' as an adjective, will ever again find favor with careful writers." If Ayres meant that the word would drop out of use, he was a bad guesser. But if he meant that careful writers would, as a matter of style, regard it wryly, he was correct. The adjectival use is acceptable, but unattractive. And usually it is unnecessary because either the context or a slight rewording will obviate it. *See also* LATE, THE.

THERE, BEGINNING A SENTENCE

There are those whose hackles rise when they read a sentence beginning "There are those. . . ." It is true that *there*, used as an expletive, is as much deadwood as the expletive *it* in a sentence beginning "It is true. . . ." Perhaps deadwood is too strong a word because, although both words are grammatically superfluous, they do serve a structural purpose in permitting the placement of the true subject in a strong position after the verb. The weakness of *there* as a sentence opener is often offset by the structure of the sentence as a whole. At least Keats thought so when he wrote, "There is not a fiercer hell than the failure in a great object." So did Longfellow when he wrote, "There is no death! What seems so is transition." And so did the translator of Genesis when he wrote, "There were giants in the earth in those days." In each of those illustrations it would be difficult to reconstruct the sentence and still retain its force. Still, unless a good rhetorical reason is present, it cannot be denied that the *there is* or *there are* opening is weak. It cannot be excused in a sentence that says, "There were no defendants present when the trial began"; the obvious and better way to phrase it would be, "No defendants were present. . . ." One legitimate use for the expletive *there* is to avoid beginning a sentence with a numeral: "There were 153 pickets outside the plant." In short, the expletive should not be tabooed, but it should be used with caution.

VERY

Books on writing style are just about unanimous in cautioning against overuse of *very* as an intensive and they will get no argument about it here. Without question, the word is overused. One of those self-same books, within two pages of its caution about *very*, discusses synonyms and says that "*teacher* and *instructor* seem very close. . . ." Which just goes to prove how insidiously the word intrudes itself. But nowhere are the cautions issued in the form of prohibitions. Obviously there are uses for the word. One is discussed under VERY PLUS PARTICIPLE in Syntax Scarecrows. And there are other constructions in which the word is well nigh essential. If someone asks, "Is Jones still alive?" the answer may properly be, "He is very much alive." You can't very well drop the word out of that reply. Any more than you can drop it out of the sentence you have just read. Those are idiomatic uses and, of course, there are others—"very true" and "very likely," for instance. In general, however, *very* as an intensive does not intensify; it is merely anemic surplus baggage. William Allen White's *Emporia Gazette*

once told of its campaign against the word in its columns as
follows:

> *If you feel you must write* very, *write* damn. *So when
> the urge for emphasis is on him, the reporter writes "It
> was a damn fine victory. I am damn tired but damn well
> —and damn excited." Then, because it is the* Emporia
> (Kan.) Gazette, *the copy desk deletes the profanity
> and the quotation reads: "It was a fine victory, I am
> tired but well—and excited." That's how the* Gazette
> *attains its restrained, simple and forceful style. Very
> simple.* *

WHICH

Grammar teachers tend to be too strict in forbidding the
use of *which* to refer to the whole idea of a preceding
clause. The only thing they need to be strict about is insistence that such a use be neither ambiguous nor clumsy. They
are right in objecting to a sentence such as this: "The man
from the city said he was not really interested in buying the
house on the riverbank, which was a bluff." But only the
ultrafinicky could object to a sentence such as this: "Snow
fell steadily and ice formed underfoot, which made the going difficult."

WIN A VICTORY

A certain newspaper copy desk chief enforced a taboo
against "win a victory" on the ground that the phrase involved a redundancy. So it does. And so does "die an honor-
able death." But just as attempting to avoid the latter
phrase would mean substituting some less suitable verb,
such as "suffer" or "meet," so escaping from "win a victory"

---

* As quoted in *Writer's Guide and Index to English*, by Porter G. Per-
rin. Scott, Foresman and Company, 1959.

means falling back on some flat or artificial verb, such as "obtain" or "achieve" or "register." In any event, writers who employ the tabooed phrase usually do not serve it up as baldly as it appears here; they are more likely to make the tautology less obvious because they write "won a hard-earned victory" or, heaven help us, "won before 10,000 cheering spectators last night a smashing victory." All this is not intended to defend the phrase, which, to be sure, is not an imaginative one, but rather to utter tsk, tsk against the taboo; the redundancy is not blatant enough to worry about.

YOU, THE READER

Used as an indefinite pronoun, *you* overcomes the remote feeling of *one*; it puts the writer into direct contact with the reader. Compare "One had better stay within the speed limit if he wants to keep out of jail" with "You had better stay within the speed limit if you want to keep out of jail." The *you* style is not only more direct but also more informal. Because of its informality, perhaps, it was not enthusiastically approved decades back. But informality in all kinds of writing has been in the ascendancy in recent times and now the indefinite *you* is accepted and widely used. Notice these typical sentences from *The Practical Stylist*, by Sheridan Baker:

"You will probably be repetitive and wordy at first—since this is our universal failing—but you will soon learn to fill your paragraph with clean and interesting details. You will develop a kind of constructional rhythm as you yourself come to a resting place at the end of your customary paragraphic frame."

A few cautions are necessary. One is not to overdo the *you* device; that same caution applies to any writing device. A second is to avoid shifting from one person to another, as

in, "You can have a drink once in a while, but one should
not drink excessively." A third is to avoid seeming to talk
down to the reader or seeming to be so personal as to be
offensive: "You may wind up in an addiction treatment
center if you insist on trying narcotics." Still a fourth caution is to avoid the *you* if it is far-fetched or unnatural:
"You may be fond of your pet camel, but the magistrate's
court doesn't think you should ride it through the garment
district." *See* ONE.

Appendix

T his is an appendix, all right, but it is more like a museum. All three partly fossilized exhibits are out of print and, by that fact alone, have a certain curiosity value. Yet their influence persists among writers to this day. Many of their strictures were valid when they were written and are just as valid now. With them this book has not been concerned. Others are so completely out of date that there was no point in mentioning them. Present-day writers are not likely to use *secesh* (secessionist) or *jackies* (sailors), nor should they be admonished to use *pantaloons* rather than *pants*. But a great many of the strictures had no validity when they were written, and naturally have none today. Still it is surprising how stubbornly some of them survive. Those are the ones that have been discussed in the preceding pages—not all of them, to be sure, but those that seem to have the most persistent grip on writers and editors.

William Cullen Bryant's list (perhaps the most sensible of the three) and that of James Gordon Bennett are addressed to newspapermen; Ambrose Bierce's is directed not only to them but also to writers in general. But since journalists not infrequently branch out into the literary field, all three have had an effect on the writing art.

WILLIAM CULLEN BRYANT'S

Index Expurgatorius

WILLIAM CULLEN BRYANT, well known as an American poet of the nineteenth century and almost as well known as a journalist, was part owner and editor in chief of the *New York Evening Post* from 1829 until his death in 1878. He had good training in Latin, which undoubtedly provided the foundation for his careful competence in English. In his *Index Expurgatorius* (presented here as it appeared in Ayres) he sought to prevent writers for the *Evening Post* from using the following:

over and above (for more than)
artiste (for artist)
aspirant
authoress
beat (for defeat)
bagging (for capturing)
balance (for remainder)
banquet (for dinner or supper)
bogus
casket (for coffin)
claimed (for asserted)
collided

commence (for begin)
compete
cortège (for procession)
cotemporary (for contemporary)
couple (for two)
darky (for negro)
day before yesterday (for the day before yesterday)
debut
decrease (as a verb)
democracy (applied to a political party)
develop (for expose)

devouring element (for fire)
donate
employé
enacted (for acted)
endorse (for approve)
en route
esq.
graduate (for is graduated)
gents (for gentlemen)
Hon.
House (for House of Representatives)
humbug
inaugurate (for begin)
in our midst
item (for particle, extract or paragraph)
is being done, and all passives of this form
jeopardize
jubilant (for rejoicing)
juvenile (for boy)
lady (for wife)
last (for latest)
lengthy (for long)
leniency (for lenity)
loafer
loan or loaned (for lend or lent)
located
majority (relating to places or circumstances, for most)
Mrs. President, Mrs. Governor, Mrs. General, and all similar titles
mutual (for common)
official (for officer)
ovation
on yesterday
over his signature
pants (for pantaloons)
parties (for persons)
partially (for partly)
past two weeks (for last two weeks and all similar expressions relating to a definite time)
poetess
portion (for part)
posted (for informed)
progress (for advance)
reliable (for trustworthy)
rendition (for performance)
repudiate (for reject or disown)
retire (as an active verb)
Rev. (for the Rev.)
role (for part)
roughs
rowdies
secesh
sensation (for noteworthy event)
standpoint (for point of view)

start (in the sense of setting
    out)
state (for say)
taboo
talent (for talents or ability)

talented
tapis
the deceased
war (for dispute or disagree-
    ment)

"Don't List"

OF THE NEW YORK HERALD
UNDER JAMES GORDON BENNETT THE YOUNGER,
ITS PROPRIETOR FROM 1867 TO 1918
FOR THE
GUIDANCE OF REPORTERS
AND COPYREADERS

COURTESY AND FAIR PLAY

Do not use any expression that will unnecessarily hold any one up to ridicule. The printing of anonymous interviews, statements and implied accusations is forbidden.

Don't say "Chinaman" for a Chinese.

Don't call a Jew a Hebrew.

Don't use "Italian" in crime stories; say foreigner. Reflections on nationalities or races are taboo.

Don't say "colored man" when you mean negro.

Don't call her an "old woman," say "aged."

OBSERVE THE LAWS OF GOOD TASTE

In writing let it be taken for granted that a person shot, stabbed or mangled will bleed. Use the word "blood" only when it is essential.

Don't say "box party" for theatre party.

Don't say a man is a "clubman."

Don't use "courtesy visit."

Don't use "visiting" in the sense of "Mr. and Mrs. Blank are visiting at Mr. Dash's villa."

Don't use "invited guest" or "invited audience."

Don't use term "dinner hostesses," "dinner dance" or "dinner guest."

Don't use "house guest," "house party" or "reception guest."

Don't use (hotel) "patron" or "guest."

Don't use "guest of honor" or "maid of honor."

Don't say a man is a "rich man" or a "magnate."

Don't use "New Yorker."

Don't say a man is a "society" man.

Don't use "week end" or "over Saturday."

Be careful in the use of the word "sick" that the context does not place upon it the possibility of an offensive construction. "Ill" is preferable.

Don't call a theatrical performance a show.

Don't use "society belle"; say "society girl" or "social leader."

Don't apply "schedule" to the movement of persons, as:—"Ambassador Bacon was scheduled to leave Vienna in the morning."

AVOID INACCURACIES OF STATEMENT

Don't say "mutual friend."

Don't refer to the "club section of the city." There is none.

Once a King or Queen always one, unless deposed, as Marie Antoinette.

Don't use "demote" for reduce. There is no word demote.

DOS AND DON'TS FOR WRITING FOR THE HERALD

Get the news, and all the news.

Outline your story before you begin to write.

Reporters will find it to their advantage to put down a

single fact, or a group of related facts, on one sheet of paper in making notes, so that they may readily and quickly arrange their material in logical sequence.

Know the subject thoroughly and think straight.

Write as well as you talk.

Avoid long and involved sentences. Make them short and crisp. Do not try to fire your whole battery of details in the introduction.

Do not tell a story more than once.

The introduction is to give to the reader a quick, illuminating flash and to hold his attention.

Tell the story clearly and forcibly and keep away from worn and hackneyed phrases. Be original even if you take a chance. Dare to be as funny as you can. Don't be afraid to say the same word over again if clearness requires it. Macaulay wasn't.

Shun the monotonous repetition of words, however, and especially avoid the use of the same word in different senses in the same paragraph.

Avoid tiresome circumlocutions; write with interest and enthusiasm. Do not compose a story so that the reader feels that the writer was watching himself go by. The highest art is that which conceals art.

Master general principles of composition.

Observe accurately, know the facts, think straight, write forcibly for on these commandments rest all the rules of newspaper English.

Below are given the official "don'ts" arranged under the rhetorical principles they violate and in alphabetical order:

AVOID TRITE AND OVERWORKED EXPRESSIONS.

Don't "hit," "slap" or "flay" in headlines.

Don't say records are "broken" or "smashed."

Don't use "probe" or "probing."

PURITY REQUIRES THE ELIMINATION OF FOREIGN WORDS UN-
LESS THERE IS NO ENGLISH WORD WHICH WILL EXPRESS THE
MEANING WHICH THE WRITER WOULD CONVEY.

"Dictograph" and "dictaphone" are patented words and
should be spelled as here given. They are Greek-Latin hy-
brids.

Don't say "per year" or "per day"; make it "per annum"
or "per diem" or "a year" or "a day." Don't mix Latin and
English.

SHUN OBSOLETE WORDS AND EXPRESSIONS. THIS IS THE TWEN-
TIETH CENTURY.

Don't use "domestic" for "servant"; it is obsolete.

TAUTOLOGY CONSISTS IN REPEATING THE THOUGHT OR
STATEMENT.

Don't use expressions akin to "silence reigned and no
sound was heard."

AVOID THE USE OF SLANG, OBSCURE TECHNICAL TERMS AND
COMMONPLACE EXPRESSIONS AND UNAUTHORIZED ABBREVI-
ATIONS IN NEWS STORIES. WHEN YOU LET YOUR FANCY FOR
SYNCOPATED ENGLISH PLAY PUT IT IN QUOTATION MARKS, OR
RESERVE IT FOR AVOWEDLY HUMOROUS FLIGHTS.

Don't clip words, as "plane" for "monoplane," "bi-
plane," &.; or "phone" for "telephone," or "auto" for
"automobile."

Don't say "fire breaks out."

Don't use "gang" or "gangster."

Don't use "hurdle" as a verb in "hurdle and ride."

Don't use "newspaper story" for "article" or "account."

Don't use "near riot."

Don't use "pants," "vest" or "full dress suit."

Don't say a place was "raided"; use "raid" as a noun.

Don't use "rush" as an adjective; no "rush orders," &.

Don't use "suicide" as a verb.

Don't say "plain clothes men."

Don't use "Zoo" for "New York Zoological Park" or the "Central Park Menagerie."

REDUNDANCY CONSISTS OF THE USE OF WORDS WHICH ARE NOT NECESSARY TO THE SENSE.

Don't use "consensus of opinion" for "consensus."

Don't use "painfully cut" or similar expressions, as though persons were "agreeably cut."

Don't say "completely destroyed."

Don't use "sword duel" or "pistol duel."

Don't use "dance music" or "promenade music."

Don't use "thrilling" as an unnecessary adjective in the context of a story as describing a situation desired to be expressed by a reporter. Let the public decide if the story is thrilling or not.

Don't sprinkle "yesterdays" throughout your story.

PRECISION CONSISTS OF THE CHOICE FROM COGNATE OR SIMILAR WORDS OF THE WORD WHICH BEST EXPRESSES THE IDEA TO BE CONVEYED. BE ACCURATE.

Don't use "casket" for "coffin."

Don't use "car" or "machine" for "automobile." Car does not mean automobile, and where automobile is meant the word automobile should be used.

Don't use "claim" for "assert." A man claims a hat; he asserts that the hat is his.

Don't use "engineer" for "engine driver."

"Hunting dogs" must be avoided; use "hounds." In an objectionable case the dogs were English setters. Use the "g" in Pekingese.

Say "hunting" when referring to the chase of game on

horseback, and "shooting" when the sportsman is afoot.

Don't say "a number"; get something more definite.

Don't use "partially" when you mean "partly."

Don't use "proposition" when you mean "proposal."

Don't say "suit was brought," say "action was begun."

PROPRIETY REQUIRES THAT WORDS OR PHRASES SHALL CON-
VEY THE EXACT AND PROPER MEANING OF THE WRITER.

Don't use "as to" for "about," "concerning" or "regarding."

Don't use "came" for "went" or "gone."

Don't use "collide" write "in collision."

Don't say "the Court said," when you mean the Judge or
Justice.

Don't say "created" when you mean "caused."

Don't use "diplomat"; use "diplomatist."

Do not use this style of the "was given" form of expression and its variations: "Admiral Dewey was given a horse"
and "Colonel Smith was presented with a sword." The
horse was given to Admiral Dewey and the sword was presented to Colonel Smith.

Don't say "had his leg broken" or "had his pocket
picked." The victims do not cause these things to be done.

Don't say Mr. Smith has "departed for Europe." "Departed" is used in "departed this life."

Don't say "disorderly house" when you mean "disreputable." A house cannot be disorderly. Do not print the
numbers of such houses.

Don't use "during" for "in." "During" means throughout the continuance of.

Don't say "groom" when you mean "bridegroom."

Don't use "epidemic" for "epizootic" in referring to a
malady widespread among animals.

Don't say "executive" session when you mean "secret" session.

Don't use "on" for "in" a street. The Metropolitan Opera House is "in" Broadway, not "on" Broadway.

Don't use "it" in reference to a baby or an animal.

Don't use "inaugurate" for "begun."

Don't say "liable" when you mean "likely."

Don't refer to the "Mayor's Cabinet." Only the President of the United States has a Cabinet.

Don't use "minister" except for diplomatists.

Don't use "Officer O'Flaherty"; say "Policeman O'Flaherty."

Don't use "over" in the sense of "more than."

Don't use "pair" for "couple."

Don't use "past" in the sense of "last"; for instance, an event that is past occurred last week or within the last few days, not in the past week or past few days.

Don't use "people" for "persons." Refer to "the people of the United States," but say "persons who saw the accident."

Don't use the word "party" for "person" except in reports of legal affairs.

Don't say "railway coaches"; say "cars." A coach is another kind of vehicle.

Don't call "rails" tracks.

Don't say "remains," say "body."

Don't use "secure" for "get," "obtain" or "procure."

Don't use "shortly" when you mean "soon" or "lengthy" for "long."

Don't say "scenes are enacted"; scenes are witnessed.

Do not use "plan" except in connection with drawn architectural or engineering plans. Do not use it as a verb. "Planned" or "planning" are taboo.

Don't say "suspect" or "suspicious person" for "suspected person."

Don't say "a wedding occurred." Explosions occur; weddings take place.

IN SHIP NEWS

DO NOT USE	USE
Prow	Bow
Wheel—when you mean	Screw
On	Onboard or aboard
Boat (except in describing a small craft propelled by oars.)	Proper name of vessel—e.g., steamship, steamboat, sloop, yawl, steam yacht, etc.
Dock (except for dry dock and large basins)	Wharf or pier
Tied up to wharf or pier	Secured to wharf or pier or made fast to wharf or pier
Knots (in describing distances)	Nautical miles. (A knot is not a distance, but a rate. Ten knots, for example, means that a vessel is making ten nautical miles an hour.)
Let down the anchor	Anchored or let go the anchor
Took up the anchor	Weighed anchor
Pilot came over the side	Pilot boarded or received pilot
Pilot left the vessel	Discharged pilot
Took out cargo	Discharged cargo
Took in cargo	Stowed cargo
Jackies	(1) Bluejackets, (2) enlisted

men, (3) sailors, or (4)
seamen and marines

Sail   In referring to the going
away of a steamship

Don't use "it" or "its" in reference to ships; a ship is of the feminine gender.

Don't use the word "liner." In designating a particular vessel the *Herald* says: "The Mauretania, of the Cunard Line."

Don't say "the yacht Corsair" or "Corsair." "The Corsair" or "yacht Corsair" is the usage. This applies to all manner of water craft.

Don't use "private yacht."

Don't say "Brooklyn" Navy Yard. It is the New York Navy Yard.

Don't use "boarded" when you mean went aboard.

Don't use "North River" for Hudson River.

Don't use "member" of the crew.

Don't say "waves"; use "seas." Waves are surface undulations; seas do damage.

AMBROSE BIERCE'S

Write It Right

A LITTLE BLACKLIST OF

LITERARY FAULTS

E XCEPT for a few years in London, Ambrose Bierce fash-
ioned most of his career as a newspaper columnist and
short-story writer in San Francisco. His caustic approach,
which is evident in this book, won him wide attention.
Write It Right was published in 1909. Four years later, at
the age of seventy-one, he departed for Mexico, where he
mysteriously disappeared.

AIMS AND THE PLAN

THE author's main purpose in this book is to teach precision in writing; and of good writing (which, essentially, is clear thinking made visible) precision is the point of capital concern. It is attained by choice of the word that accurately and adequately expresses what the writer has in mind, and by exclusion of that which either denotes or connotes something else. As Quintilian puts it, the writer should so write that his reader not only may, but must, understand.

Few words have more than one literal and serviceable meaning, however many metaphorical, derivative, related, or even unrelated, meanings lexicographers may think it worth while to gather from all sorts and conditions of men, with which to bloat their absurd and misleading dictionaries. This actual and serviceable meaning—not always determined by derivation, and seldom by popular usage—is the one affirmed, according to his light, by the author of this little manual of solecisms. Narrow etymons of the mere scholar and loose locutions of the ignorant are alike denied a standing.

The plan of the book is more illustrative than expository, the aim being to use the terms of etymology and syntax as little as is compatible with clarity, familiar example being more easily apprehended than technical precept. When both are employed the precept is commonly given after the example has prepared the student to apply it, not only to the matter in mind, but to similar matters not mentioned. Everything in quotation marks is to be understood as disapproved.

Not all locutions blacklisted herein are always to be reprobated as universal outlaws. Excepting in the case of capital offenders—expressions ancestrally vulgar or irreclaimably degenerate—absolute proscription is possible as to serious composition only; in other forms the writer must rely on his sense of values and the fitness of things. While it is true that some colloquialisms and, with less of license, even some slang, may be sparingly employed in light literature, for point, piquancy or any of the purposes of the skilled writer sensible to the necessity and charm of keeping at least one foot on the ground, to others the virtue of restraint may be commended as distinctly superior to the joy of indulgence.

Precision is much, but not all; some words and phrases are disallowed on the ground of taste. As there are neither standards nor arbiters of taste, the book can do little more than reflect that of its author, who is far indeed from professing impeccability. In neither taste nor precision is any man's practice a court of last appeal, for writers all, both great and small, are habitual sinners against the light; and their accuser is cheerfully aware that his own work will supply (as in making this book it has supplied) many "awful examples"—his later work less abundantly, he hopes, than his earlier. He nevertheless believes that this does not disqualify him for showing by other instances than his own how not to write. The infallible teacher is still in the forest primeval, throwing seeds to the white blackbirds.

A. B.

THE BLACKLIST

A for *An*. "A hotel." "A heroic man." Before an unaccented aspirate use an. The contrary usage in this country comes of too strongly stressing our aspirates.

Action for *Act*. "In wrestling, a blow is a reprehensible action." A blow is not an action but an act. An action may consist of many acts.

Admission for *Admittance.* "The price of admission is one dollar."

Admit for *Confess.* To admit is to concede something affirmed. An unaccused offender cannot admit his guilt.

Adopt. "He adopted a disguise." One may adopt a child, or an opinion, but a disguise is assumed.

Advisedly for *Advertently, Intentionally.* "It was done advisedly" should mean that it was done after advice.

Afford. It is not well to say "the fact affords a reasonable presumption"; "the house afforded ample accommodation." The fact supplies a reasonable presumption. The house offered, or gave, ample accommodation.

Afraid. Do not say, "I am afraid it will rain." Say, I fear that it will rain.

Afterwards for *Afterward.*

Aggravate for *Irritate.* "He aggravated me by his insolence." To aggravate is to augment the disagreeableness of something already disagreeable, or the badness of something bad. But a person cannot be aggravated, even if disagreeable or bad. Women are singularly prone to misuse of this word.

All of. "He gave all of his property." The words are contradictory: an entire thing cannot be of itself. Omit the preposition.

Alleged. "The alleged murderer." One can allege a murder, but not a murderer; a crime, but not a criminal. A man that is merely suspected of crime would not, in any case, be an alleged criminal, for an allegation is a definite and positive statement. In their tiresome addiction to this use of alleged, the newspapers, though having mainly in mind the danger of libel suits, can urge in further justification the lack of any other single word that exactly expresses their meaning; but the fact that a mud-puddle supplies the shortest route is not a compelling reason for walking through it. One can go around.

Allow for *Permit.* "I allow you to go." Precision is better attained by saying permit, for allow has other meanings.

Allude to for *Mention.* What is alluded to is not mentioned, but referred to indirectly. Originally, the word implied a playful, or sportive, reference. That meaning is gone out of it.

And so. And yet. "And so they were married." "And yet a woman." Omit the conjunction.

And which. And who. These forms are incorrect unless the relative pronoun has been used previously in the sentence. "The colt, spirited and strong, and which was unbroken, escaped from the pasture." "John Smith, one of our leading merchants, and who fell from a window yesterday, died this morning." Omit the conjunction.

Antecedents for *Personal History.* Antecedents are predecessors.

Anticipate for *Expect.* "I anticipate trouble." To anticipate is to act on an expectation in a way to promote or forestall the event expected.

Anxious for *Eager.* "I was anxious to go." Anxious should not be followed by an infinitive. Anxiety is contemplative; eagerness, alert for action.

Appreciate for *Highly Value.* In the sense of value, it means value justly, not highly. In another and preferable sense it means to increase in value.

Approach. "The juror was approached"; that is, overtures were made to him with a view to bribing him. As there is no other single word for it, approach is made to serve, figuratively; and being graphic, it is not altogether objectionable.

Appropriated for *Took.* "He appropriated his neighbor's

horse to his own use." To appropriate is to set apart, as a sum of money, for a special purpose.

Approve of for *Approve.* There is no sense in making approve an intransitive verb.

Apt for *Likely.* "One is apt to be mistaken." Apt means facile, felicitous, ready, and the like; but even the dictionary-makers cannot persuade a person of discriminating taste to accept it as synonymous with likely.

Around for *About.* "The débris of battle lay around them." "The huckster went around, crying his wares." Around carries the concept of circularity.

Article. A good and useful word, but used without meaning by shopkeepers; as, "A good article of vinegar," for a good vinegar.

As for *That,* or *If.* "I do not know as he is living." This error is not very common among those who can write at all, but one sometimes sees it in high place.

As—as for *So—as.* "He is not as good as she." Say, not so good. In affirmative sentences the rule is different: He is as good as she.

As for for *As to.* "As for me, I am well." Say, as to me.

At Auction for *by Auction.* "The goods were sold at auction."

At for *By.* "She was shocked at his conduct." This very common solecism is without excuse.

Attain for *Accomplish.* "By diligence we attain our purpose." A purpose is accomplished; success is attained.

Authoress. A needless word—as needless as "poetess."

Avocation for *Vocation.* A vocation is, literally, a calling; that is, a trade or profession. An avocation is something that calls one away from it. If I say that farming is some one's avocation I mean that he practises it, not regularly, but at odd times.

Avoid for *Avert.* "By displaying a light the skipper

avoided a collision." To avoid is to shun; the skipper could have avoided a collision only by getting out of the way.

Avoirdupois for *Weight*. Mere slang.

Back of for *Behind, At the Back of*. "Back of law is force."

Backwards for *Backward*.

Badly for *Bad*. "I feel badly." "He looks badly." The former sentence implies defective nerves of sensation, the latter, imperfect vision. Use the adjective.

Balance for *Remainder* "The balance of my time is given to recreation." In this sense balance is a commercial word, and relates to accounting.

Banquet. A good enough word in its place, but its place is the dictionary. Say, dinner.

Bar for *Bend*. "Bar sinister." There is no such thing in heraldry as a bar sinister.

Because for *For*. "I knew it was night, because it was dark." "He will not go, because he is ill."

Bet for *Betted*. The verb to bet forms its preterite regularly, as do wet, wed, knit, quit and others that are commonly misconjugated. It seems that we clip our short words more than we do our long.

Body for *Trunk*. "The body lay here, the head there." The body is the entire physical person (as distinguished from the soul, or mind) and the head is a part of it. As distinguished from head, trunk may include the limbs, but anatomically it is the torso only.

Bogus for *Counterfeit*, or *False*. The word is slang; keep it out.

Both. This word is frequently misplaced; as, "A large mob, both of men and women." Say, of both men and women.

Both alike. "They are both alike." Say, they are alike. One of them could not be alike.

Brainy. Pure slang, and singularly disagreeable.

Bug for *Beetle*, or for anything. Do not use it.

Business for *Right.* "He has no business to go there."

Build for *Make.* "Build a fire." "Build a canal." Even "build a tunnel" is not unknown, and probably if the woodchuck is skilled in the American tongue he speaks of building a hole.

But. By many writers this word (in the sense of except) is regarded as a preposition, to be followed by the objective case: "All went but him." It is not a preposition and may take either the nominative or objective case, to agree with the subject or the object of the verb. All went but he. The natives killed all but him.

But what. "I did not know but what he was an enemy." Omit what. If condemnation of this dreadful locution seem needless bear the matter in mind in your reading and you will soon be of a different opinion.

By for *Of.* "A man by the name of Brown." Say, of the name. Better than either form is: a man named Brown.

Calculated for *Likely.* "The bad weather is calculated to produce sickness." Calculated implies calculation, design.

Can for *May.* "Can I go fishing?" "He can call on me if he wishes to."

Candidate for *Aspirant.* In American politics, one is not a candidate for an office until formally named (nominated) for it by a convention, or otherwise, as provided by law or custom. So when a man who is moving Heaven and Earth to procure the nomination protests that he is "not a candidate" he tells the truth in order to deceive.

Cannot for *Can.* "I cannot but go." Say, I can but go.

Capable. "Men are capable of being flattered." Say, susceptible to flattery. "Capable of being refuted." Vulnerable to refutation. Unlike capacity, capability is not passive, but active. We are capable of doing, not of having something done to us.

Capacity for *Ability*. "A great capacity for work." Capacity is receptive; ability, potential. A sponge has capacity for water; the hand, ability to squeeze it out.

Casket for *Coffin*. A needless euphemism affected by undertakers.

Casualties for *Losses* in Battle. The essence of casualty is accident, absence of design. Death and wounds in battle are produced otherwise, are expectable and expected, and, by the enemy, intentional.

Chance for *Opportunity*. "He had a good chance to succeed."

Chin Whiskers. The whisker grows on the cheek, not the chin.

Chivalrous. The word is popularly used in the Southern States only, and commonly has reference to men's manner toward women. Archaic, stilted and fantastic.

Citizen for *Civilian*. A soldier may be a citizen, but is not a civilian.

Claim for *Affirm*. "I claim that he is elected." To claim is to assert ownership.

Clever for *Obliging*. In this sense the word was once in general use in the United States, but is now seldom heard and life here is less insupportable.

Climb down. In climbing one ascends.

Coat for *Coating*. "A coat of paint, or varnish." If we coat something we produce a coating, not a coat.

Collateral Descendant. There can be none: a "collateral descendant" is not a descendant.

Colonel, Judge, Governor, etc., for *Mister*. Give a man a title only if it belongs to him, and only while it belongs to him.

Combine for *Combination*. The word, in this sense, has something of the meaning of conspiracy, but there is no justification for it as a noun, in any sense.

Commence for *Begin*. This is not actually incorrect, but —well, it is a matter of taste.

Commencement for *Termination*. A contribution to our noble tongue by its scholastic conservators, "commencement day" being their name for the last day of the collegiate year. It is ingeniously defended on the ground that on that day those on whom degrees are bestowed commence to hold them. Lovely!

Commit Suicide. Instead of "He committed suicide," say, He killed himself, or, He took his life. For married we do not say "committed matrimony." Unfortunately most of us do say, "got married," which is almost as bad. For lack of a suitable verb we just sometimes say committed this or that, as in the instance of bigamy, for the verb to bigam is a blessing that is still in store for us.

Compare with for *Compare to*. "He had the immodesty to compare himself with Shakespeare." Nothing necessarily immodest in that. Comparison with may be for observing a difference; comparison to affirms a similarity.

Complected. Anticipatory past participle of the verb "to complect." Let us wait for that.

Conclude for *Decide*. "I concluded to go to town." Having concluded a course of reasoning (implied), I decided to go to town. A decision is supposed to be made at the conclusion of a course of reasoning, but is not the conclusion itself. Conversely, the conclusion of a syllogism is not a decision, but an inference.

Connection. "In this connection I should like to say a word or two." In connection with this matter.

Conscious for *Aware*. "The King was conscious of the

conspiracy." We are conscious of what we feel; aware of what we know.

Consent for *Assent.* "He consented to that opinion." To consent is to agree to a proposal; to assent is to agree with a proposition.

Conservative for *Moderate.* "A conservative estimate"; "a conservative forecast"; "a conservative statement," and so on. These and many other abuses of the word are of recent growth in the newspapers and "halls of legislation." Having been found to have several meanings, conservative seems to be thought to mean everything.

Continually and *Continuously.* It seems that these words should have the same meaning, but in their use by good writers there is a difference. What is done continually is not done all the time, but continuous action is without interruption. A loquacious fellow, who nevertheless finds time to eat and sleep, is continually talking; but a great river flows continuously.

Convoy for *Escort.* "A man-of-war acted as convoy to the flotilla." The flotilla is the convoy, the man-of-war the escort.

Couple for *Two.* For two things to be a couple they must be of one general kind, and their number unimportant to the statement made of them. It would be weak to say, "He gave me only one, although he took a couple for himself." Couple expresses indifference to the exact number, as does several. That is true, even in the phrase, a married couple, for the number is carried in the adjective and needs no emphasis.

Created for *First Performed.* Stage slang. "Burbage created the part of Hamlet." What was it that its author did to it?

Critically for *Seriously.* "He has long been critically ill."

A patient is critically ill only at the crisis of his disease.

Criticise for *Condemn*, or *Disparage*. Criticism is not necessarily censorious; it may approve.

Cunning for *Amusing*. Usually said of a child, or pet. This is pure Americanese, as is its synonym, "cute."

Curious for *Odd*, or *Singular*. To be curious is to have an inquiring mind, or mood—curiosity.

Custom for *Habit*. Communities have customs; individuals, habits—commonly bad ones.

Decease for *Die*.

Decidedly for *Very*, or *Certainly*. "It is decidedly cold."

Declared for *Said*. To a newspaper reporter no one seems ever to say anything; all "declare." Like "alleged" (which see) the word is tiresome exceedingly.

Defalcation for *Default*. A defalcation is a cutting off, a subtraction; a default is a failure in duty.

Definitely for *Definitively*. "It was definitely decided." Definitely means precisely, with exactness; definitively means finally, conclusively.

Deliver. "He delivered an oration," or "delivered a lecture." Say, He made an oration, or gave a lecture.

Demean for *Debase* or *Degrade*. "He demeaned himself by accepting charity." The word relates, not to meanness, but to demeanor, conduct, behavior. One may demean oneself with dignity and credit.

Demise for *Death*. Usually said of a person of note. Demise means the lapse, as by death, of some authority, distinction or privilege, which passes to another than the one that held it; as the demise of the Crown.

Democracy for *Democratic Party*. One could as properly call the Christian Church "the Christianity."

Dépôt for *Station*. "Railroad dépôt." A dépôt is a place of deposit; as, a dépôt of supply for an army.

Deprivation for *Privation*. "The mendicant showed the

effects of deprivation." Deprivation refers to the act of de-
priving, taking away from; privation is the state of destitu-
tion, of not having.

Dilapidated for *Ruined.* Said of a building, or other
structure. But the word is from the Latin *lapis,* a stone, and
cannot properly be used of any but a stone structure.

Directly for *Immediately.* "I will come directly" means
that I will come by the most direct route.

Dirt for *Earth, Soil,* or *Gravel.* A most disagreeable
Americanism, discredited by general (and Presidential)
use. "Make the dirt fly." Dirt means filth.

Distinctly for *Distinctively.* "The custom is distinctly
Oriental." Distinctly is plainly; distinctively, in a way to
distinguish one thing from others.

Donate for *Give.* Good American, but not good English.

Doubtlessly. A doubly adverbial form, like "illy."

Dress for *Gown.* Not so common as it was a few years
ago. Dress means the entire costume.

Each Other for *One Another.* "The three looked at each
other." That is, each looked at the other. But there were
more than one other; so we should say they looked at one
another, which means that each looked at another. Of two,
say each other; of more than two, one another.

Edify for *Please,* or *Entertain.* Edify means to build; it
has, therefore, the sense of uplift, improvement—usually
moral, or spiritual.

Electrocution. To one having even an elementary
knowledge of Latin grammar this word is no less than disgusting, and the thing meant by it is felt to be altogether
too good for the word's inventor.

Empty for *Vacant.* Say, an empty bottle; but, a vacant
house.

Employé. Good French, but bad English. Say, em-
ployee.

Endorse for *Approve.* To endorse is to write upon the back of, or to sign the promissory note of another. It is a commercial word, having insufficient dignity for literary use. You may endorse a check, but you approve a policy, or statement.

Endways. A corruption of endwise.

Entitled for *Authorized, Privileged.* "The man is not entitled to draw rations." Say, entitled to rations. Entitled is not to be followed by an infinitive.

Episode for *Occurrence, Event,* etc. Properly, an episode is a narrative that is a subordinate part of another narrative. An occurrence considered by itself is not an episode.

Equally as for *Equally.* "This is equally as good." Omit as. "He was of the same age, and equally as tall." Say, equally tall.

Equivalent for *Equal.* "My salary is equivalent to yours."

Essential for *Necessary.* This solecism is common among the best writers of this country and England. "It is essential to go early"; "Irrigation is essential to cultivation of arid lands," and so forth. One thing is essential to another thing only if it is of the essence of it—an important and indispensable part of it, determining its nature; the soul of it.

Even for *Exact.* "An even dozen."

Every for *Entire, Full.* "The president had every confidence in him."

Every for *Ever.* "Every now and then." This is nonsense: there can be no such thing as a now and then, nor, of course, a number of now and thens. Now and then is itself bad enough, reversing as it does the sequence of things, but it is idiomatic and there is no quarreling with it. But "every" is here a corruption of ever, meaning repeatedly, continually.

Ex. "Ex-President," "an ex-convict," and the like. Say,

former. In England one may say, Mr. Roosevelt, sometime President; though the usage is a trifle archaic.

Example for *Problem.* A heritage from the text-books. "An example in arithmetic." An equally bad word for the same thing is "sum": "Do the sum," for Solve the problem.

Excessively for *Exceedingly.* "The disease is excessively painful." "The weather is excessively cold." Anything that is painful at all is excessively so. Even a slight degree or small amount of what is disagreeable or injurious is excessive—that is to say, redundant, superfluous, not required.

Executed. "The condemned man was executed." He was hanged, or otherwise put to death; it is the sentence that is executed.

Executive for *Secret.* An executive session of a deliberative body is a session for executive business, as distinguished from legislative. It is commonly secret, but a secret session is not necessarily executive.

Expect for *Believe,* or *Suppose.* "I expect he will go." Say, I believe (suppose or think) he will go; or, I expect him to go.

Expectorate for *Spit.* The former word is frequently used, even in laws and ordinances, as a euphemism for the latter. It not only means something entirely different, but to one with a Latin ear is far more offensive.

Experience for *Suffer,* or *Undergo.* "The sinner experienced a change of heart." This will do if said lightly or mockingly. It does not indicate a serious frame of mind in the speaker.

Extend for *Proffer.* "He extended an invitation." One does not always hold out an invitation in one's hand; it may be spoken or sent.

Fail. "He failed to note the hour." That implies that he tried to note it, but did not succeed. Failure carries always the sense of endeavor; when there has been no endeavor there is no failure. A falling stone cannot fail to strike you, for it does not try; but a marksman firing at you may fail to hit you; and I hope he always will.

Favor for *Resemble*. "The child favors its father."

Feel of for *Feel*. "The doctor felt of the patient's head." "Smell of" and "taste of" are incorrect too.

Feminine for *Female*. "A feminine member of the club." Feminine refers, not to sex proper, but to gender, which may be defined as the sex of words. The same is true of masculine.

Fetch for *Bring*. Fetching includes, not only bringing, but going to get—going for and returning with. You may bring what you did not go for.

Finances for *Wealth*, or *Pecuniary Resources*.

Financial for *Pecuniary*. "His financial reward"; "he is financially responsible," and so forth.

Firstly. If this word could mean anything it would mean firstlike, whatever that might mean. The ordinal numbers should have no abverbial form: "firstly," "secondly," and the rest are words without meaning.

Fix. This is, in America, a word-of-all-work, most frequently meaning repair, or prepare. Do not so use it.

Forebears for *Ancestors*. The word is sometimes spelled forbears, a worse spelling than the other, but not much. If used at all it should be spelled *forebeers*, for it means those who have *been* before. A forebe-er is one who fore-was. Considered in any way, it is a senseless word.

Forecasted. For this abominable word we are indebted to the weather bureau—at least it was not sent upon us until that affliction was with us. Let us hope that it may some day be losted from the language.

Former and *Latter*. Indicating the first and the second of things previously named, these words are unobjectionable if not too far removed from the names that they stand for. If they are they confuse, for the reader has to look back to the names. Use them sparingly.

Funeral Obsequies. Tautological. Say, obsequies; the word is now used in none but a funereal sense.

Fully for *Definitively,* or *Finally.* "After many preliminary examinations he was fully committed for trial." The adverb is meaningless: a defendant is never partly committed for trial. This is a solecism to which lawyers are addicted. And sometimes they have been heard to say "fullied."

Funds for *Money.* "He was out of funds." Funds are not money in general, but sums of money or credit available for particular purposes.

Furnish for *Provide,* or *Supply.* "Taxation furnished the money." A pauper may furnish a house if some one will provide the furniture, or the money to buy it. "His flight furnishes a presumption of guilt." It supplies it.

Generally for *Usually.* "The winds are generally high." "A fool is generally vain." This misuse of the word appears to come of abbreviating: Generally speaking, the weather is bad. A fool, to speak generally, is vain.

Gent for *Gentleman.* Vulgar exceedingly.

Genteel. This word, meaning polite, or well mannered, was once in better repute than it is now, and its noun, gentility, is still not infrequently found in the work of good writers. Genteel is most often used by those who write, as the Scotchman of the anecdote joked—wi' deeficulty.

Gentleman. It is not possible to teach the correct use of this overworked word: one must be bred to it. Everybody knows that it is not synonymous with man, but among the "genteel" and those ambitious to be thought "genteel" it is commonly so used in discourse too formal for the word "gent." To use the word gentleman correctly, be one.

Genuine for *Authentic,* or *Veritable.* "A genuine document," "a genuine surprise," and the like.

Given. "The soldier was given a rifle." What was given is the rifle, not the soldier. "The house was given a coat (coating) of paint." Nothing can be "given" anything.

Goatee. In this country goatee is frequently used for a tuft of beard on the point of the chin—what is sometimes called "an imperial," apparently because the late Emperor Napoleon III wore his beard so. His Majesty the Goat is graciously pleased to wear his beneath the chin.

Got Married for *Married.* If this is correct we should say, also, "got dead" for died; one expression is as good as the other.

Gotten for *Got.* This has gone out of good use, though in such compounded words as begotten and misbegotten it persists respectably.

Graduated for *Was Graduated.*

Gratuitous for *Unwarranted.* "A gratuitous assertion." Gratuitous means without cost.

Grueling. Used chiefly by newspaper reporters; as, "He was subjected to a grueling cross-examination." "It was grueling weather." Probably a corruption of grilling.

Gubernatorial. Eschew it; it is not English, is needless and bombastic. Leave it to those who call a political office a "chair." "Gubernatorial chair" is good enough for them. So is hanging.

Had Better for *Would Better.* This is not defensible as an idiom, as those who always used it before their attention was directed to it take the trouble to point out. It comes of such contractions as he'd for he would, I'd for I would. These clipped words are erroneously restored as "he had," "I had." So we have such monstrosities as "He had better beware," "I had better go."

Hail for *Come.* "He hails from Chicago." This is sea speech, and comes from the custom of hailing passing ships. It will not do for serious discourse.

Have Got for *Have.* "I have got a good horse" directs attention rather to the act of getting than to the state of having, and represents the capture as recently completed.

Head over Heels. A transposition of words hardly less surprising than (to the person most concerned) the mischance that it fails to describe. What is meant is heels over head.

Healthy for *Wholesome.* "A healthy climate." "A healthy occupation." Only a living thing can be healthy.

Helpmeet for *Helpmate.* In Genesis Adam's wife is called "an help meet for him," that is, fit for him. The ridiculous word appears to have had no other origin.

Hereafter for *Henceforth.* Hereafter means at some time in the future; henceforth, always in the future. The penitent who promises to be good hereafter commits himself to the performance of a single good act, not to a course of good conduct.

Honeymoon. Moon here means month, so it is incorrect to say, "a week's honeymoon," or, "Their honeymoon lasted a year."

Horseflesh for *Horses.* A singularly senseless and disagreeable word which, when used, as it commonly is, with reference to hippophilism, savors rather more of the spit than of the spirit.

Humans as a Noun. We have no single word having the general yet limited meaning that this is sometimes used to express—a meaning corresponding to that of the word animals, as the word men would if it included women and children. But there is time enough to use two words.

Hung for *Hanged.* A bell, or a curtain, is hung, but a

man is hanged. Hung is the junior form of the participle, and is now used for everything but man. Perhaps it is our reverence for the custom of hanging men that sacredly preserves the elder form—as some, even, of the most zealous American spelling reformers still respect the u in Saviour.

Hurry for *Haste* and *Hasten.* To hurry is to hasten in a more or less disorderly manner. Hurry is misused, also, in another sense: "There is no hurry"—meaning, There is no reason for haste.

Hurt for *Harm.* "It does no hurt." To be hurt is to feel pain, but one may be harmed without knowing it. To spank a child, or flout a fool, hurts without harming.

Idea for *Thought, Purpose, Expectation,* etc. "I had no idea that it was so cold." "When he went abroad it was with no idea of remaining."

Identified with. "He is closely identified with the temperance movement." Say, connected.

Ilk for *Kind.* "Men of that ilk." This Scotch word has a narrowly limited and specific meaning. It relates to an ancestral estate having the same name as the person spoken of. Macdonald of that ilk means, Macdonald of Macdonald. The phrase quoted above is without meaning.

Illy for *Ill.* There is no such word as illy, for ill itself is an adverb.

Imaginary Line. The adjective is needless. Geometrically, every line is imaginary; its graphic representation is a mark. True the text-books say, draw a line, but in a mathematical sense the line already exists; the drawing only makes its course visible.

In for *Into.* "He was put in jail." "He went in the house." A man may be in jail, or be in a house, but when the act of entrance—the movement of something from the outside to the inside of another thing—is related the correct word is into if the latter thing is named.

Inaugurate for *Begin, Establish,* etc. Inauguration implies some degree of formality and ceremony.

Incumbent for *Obligatory.* "It was incumbent upon me to relieve him." Infelicitous and work-worn. Say, It was my duty, or, if enamored of that particular metaphor, It lay upon me.

Individual. As a noun, this word means something that cannot be considered as divided, a unit. But it is incorrect to call a man, woman or child an individual, except with reference to mankind, to society or to a class of persons. It will not do to say, "An individual stood in the street," when no mention nor allusion has been made, nor is going to be made, to some aggregate of individuals considered as a whole.

Indorse. See *Endorse.*

Insane Asylum. Obviously an asylum cannot be unsound in mind. Say, asylum for the insane.

In Spite of. In most instances it is better to say despite.

Inside of. Omit the preposition.

Insignificant for *Trivial,* or *Small.* Insignificant means not signifying anything, and should be used only in contrast, expressed or implied, with something that is important for what it implies. The bear's tail may be insignificant to a naturalist tracing the animal's descent from an earlier species, but to the rest of us, not concerned with the matter, it is merely small.

Insoluble for *Unsolvable.* Use the former word for material substances, the latter for problems.

Inst., Prox., Ult. These abbreviations of *instante mense* (in the present month), *proximo mense* (in the next month) and *ultimo mense* (in the last month), are serviceable enough in commercial correspondence, but, like A. M., P. M. and many other contractions of Latin words, could profitably be spared from literature.

Integrity for *Honesty*. The word means entireness, wholeness. It may be rightly used to affirm possession of all the virtues, that is, unity of moral character.

Involve for *Entail*. "Proof of the charges will involve his dismissal." Not at all; it will entail it. To involve is, literally, to infold, not to bring about, nor cause to ensue. An unofficial investigation, for example, may involve character and reputation, but the ultimate consequence is entailed. A question, in the parliamentary sense, may involve a principle; its settlement one way or another may entail expense, or injury to interests. An act may involve one's honor and entail disgrace.

It for *So*. "Going into the lion's cage is dangerous; you should not do it." Do so is the better expression, as a rule, for the word it is a pronoun, meaning a thing, or object, and therefore incapable of being done. Colloquially we may say do it, or do this, or do that, but in serious written discourse greater precision is desirable, and is better obtained, in most cases, by use of the adverb.

Item for *Brief Article*. Commonly used of a narrative in a newspaper. Item connotes an aggregate of which it is a unit—one thing of many. Hence it suggests more than we may wish to direct attention to.

Jackies for *Sailors*. Vulgar, and especially offensive to seamen.

Jeopardize for *Imperil*, or *Endanger*. The correct word is jeopard, but in any case there is no need for anything so farfetched and stilted.

Juncture. Juncture means a joining, a junction; its use to signify a time, however critical a time, is absurd. "At this juncture the woman screamed." In reading that account of it we scream too.

Just Exactly. Nothing is gained in strength nor precision by this kind of pleonasm. Omit just.

Juvenile for *Child.* This needless use of the adjective for the noun is probably supposed to be humorous, like "canine" for dog, "optic" for eye, "anatomy" for body, and the like. Happily the offense is not very common.

Kind of a for *Kind of.* "He was that kind of a man." Say that kind of man. Man here is generic, and a genus comprises many kinds. But there cannot be more than one kind of one thing. *Kind of* followed by an adjective, as, "kind of good," is almost too gross for censure.

Landed Estate for *Property in Land.* Dreadful!

Last and *Past.* "Last week." "The past week." Neither is accurate: a week cannot be the last if another is already begun; and all weeks except this one are past. Here two wrongs seem to make a right: we can say the week last past. But will we? I trow not.

Later on. On is redundant; say, later.

Laundry. Meaning a place where clothing is washed, this word cannot mean, also, clothing sent there to be washed.

Lay (to place) for *Lie* (to recline). "The ship lays on her side." A more common error is made in the past tense, as, "He laid down on the grass." The confusion comes of the identity of a present tense of the transitive verb to lay and the past tense of the intransitive verb to lie.

Leading Question. A leading question is not necessarily an important one; it is one that is so framed as to suggest, or lead to, the answer desired. Few others than lawyers use the term correctly.

Lease. To say of a man that he leases certain premises leaves it doubtful whether he is lessor or lessee. Being ambiguous, the word should be used with caution.

Leave for *Go away.* "He left yesterday." Leave is a transitive verb; name the place of departure.

Leave for *Let.* "Leave it alone." By this many persons

mean, not that it is to be left in solitude, but that it is to be untouched, or unmolested.

Lengthways for *Lengthwise.*

Lengthy. Usually said in disparagement of some wearisome discourse. It is no better than breadthy, or thicknessy.

Leniency for *Lenity.* The words are synonymous, but the latter is the better.

Less for *Fewer.* "The regiment had less than five hundred men." Less relates to quantity, fewer, to number.

Limited for *Small, Inadequate,* etc. "The army's operations were confined to a limited area." "We had a limited supply of food." A large area and an adequate supply would also be limited. Everything that we know about is limited.

Liable for *Likely.* "Man is liable to err." Man is not liable to err, but to error. Liable should be followed, not by an infinitive, but by a preposition.

Like for *As,* or *As if.* "The matter is now like it was." "The house looked like it would fall."

Likely for *Probably.* "He will likely be elected." If likely is thought the better word (and in most cases it is) put it this way: "It is likely that he will be elected," or, "He is likely to be elected."

Line for *Kind,* or *Class.* "This line of goods." Leave the word to "salesladies" and "salesgentlemen." "That line of business." Say, that business.

Literally for *Figuratively.* "The stream was literally alive with fish." "His eloquence literally swept the audience from its feet." It is bad enough to exaggerate, but to affirm the truth of the exaggeration is intolerable.

Loan for *Lend.* "I loaned him ten dollars." We lend, but the act of lending, or, less literally, the thing lent, is a loan.

Locate. "After many removals the family located at Smithville." Some dictionaries give locate as an intransitive verb having that meaning, but—well, dictionaries are funny.

Lots, or *a Lot,* for *Much,* or *Many.* "Lots of things." "A lot of talk."

Love for *Like.* "I love to travel." "I love apples." Keep the stronger word for a stronger feeling.

Lunch for *Luncheon.* But do not use luncheon as a verb.

Mad for *Angry.* An Americanism of lessening prevalence. It is probable that anger is a kind of madness (insanity), but that is not what the misusers of the word mad mean to affirm.

Maintain for *Contend.* "The senator maintained that the tariff was iniquitous." He maintained it only if he proved it.

Majority for *Plurality.* Concerning votes cast in an election, a majority is more than half the total; a plurality is the excess of one candidate's votes over another's. Commonly the votes compared are those for the successful candidate and those for his most nearly successful competitor.

Make for *Earn.* "He makes fifty dollars a month by manual labor."

Mansion for *Dwelling,* or *House.* Usually mere hyperbole, a lamentable fault of our national literature. Even our presidents, before Roosevelt, called their dwelling the Executive Mansion.

Masculine for *Male.* See *Feminine.*

Mend for *Repair.* "They mended the road." To mend is to repair, but to repair is not always to mend. A stocking is mended, a road repaired.

Meet for *Meeting.* This belongs to the language of sport, which persons of sense do not write—nor read.

Militate. "Negligence militates against success." If "militate" meant anything it would mean fight, but there is no such word.

Mind for *Obey*. This is a reasonless extension of one legitimate meaning of mind, namely, to heed, to give attention.

Minus for *Lacking*, or *Without*. "After the battle he was minus an ear." It is better in serious composition to avoid such alien words as have vernacular equivalents.

Mistaken for *Mistake*. "You are mistaken." For whom? Say, You mistake.

Monarch for *King, Emperor*, or *Sovereign*. Not only hyperbolical, but inaccurate. There is not a monarch in Christendom.

Moneyed for *Wealthy*. "The moneyed men of New York." One might as sensibly say, "The cattled men of Texas," or, "The lobstered men of the fish market."

Most for *Almost*. "The apples are most all gone." "The returning travelers were most home."

Moved for *Removed*. "The family has moved to another house." "The Joneses were moving."

Mutual. By this word we express a reciprocal relation. It implies exchange, a giving and taking, not a mere possessing in common. There can be a mutual affection, or a mutual hatred, but not a mutual friend, nor a mutual horse.

Name for *Title and Name*. "His name was Mr. Smith." Surely no babe was ever christened Mister.

Necessaries for *Means*. "Bread and meat are necessaries of life." Not so; they are the mere means, for one can, and many do, live comfortably without them. Food and drink are necessaries of life, but particular kinds of food and drink are not.

Necessities for *Necessaries*. "Necessities of life are those things without which we cannot live."

Née. Feminine of *né*, born. "Mrs. Jones, *née* Lucy Smith." She could hardly have been christened before her birth. If you must use the French word say, *née* Smith.

Negotiate. From the Latin *negotium.* It means, as all know, to fix the terms for a transaction, to bargain. But when we say, "The driver negotiated a difficult turn of the road," or, "The chauffeur negotiated a hill," we speak nonsense.

Neither—or for *Neither—nor.* "Neither a cat or fish has wool." Always after neither use nor.

New Beginner for *Beginner.*

Nice for *Good,* or *Agreeable.* "A nice girl." Nice means fastidious, delicately discriminative, and the like. Pope uses the word admirably of a dandy who was skilled in the nice conduct [management] of a clouded cane.

Noise for *Sound.* "A noise like a flute"; "a noise of twittering birds," etc. A noise is a loud or disagreeable sound, or combination or succession of sounds.

None. Usually, and in most cases, singular; as, None has come. But it is not singular because it always means not one, for frequently it does not, as, The bottle was full of milk, but none is left. When it refers to numbers, not quantity, popular usage stubbornly insists that it is plural, and at least one respectable authority says that as a singular it is offensive. One is sorry to be offensive to a good man.

No Use. "He tried to smile, but it was no use." Say, of no use, or, less colloquially, in vain.

Novel for *Romance.* In a novel there is at least an apparent attention to considerations of probability; it is a narrative of what might occur. Romance flies with a free wing and owns no allegiance to likelihood. Both are fiction, both works of imagination, but should not be confounded. They are as distinct as beast and bird.

Numerous for *Many.* Rightly used, numerous relates to numbers, but does not imply a great number. A correct use is seen in the term numerous verse—verse consisting of poetic numbers; that is, rhythmical feet.

Obnoxious for *Offensive*. Obnoxious means exposed to evil. A soldier in battle is obnoxious to danger.

Occasion for *Induce*, or *Cause*. "His arrival occasioned a great tumult." As a verb, the word is needless and unpleasing.

Occasional Poems. These are not, as so many authors and compilers seem to think, poems written at irregular and indefinite intervals, but poems written for *occasions*, such as anniversaries, festivals, celebrations and the like.

Of Any for *Of All*. "The greatest poet of any that we have had."

Offhanded and *Offhandedly*. Offhand is both adjective and adverb; these are bastard forms.

On the Street. A street comprises the roadway and the buildings at each side. Say, in the street. He lives in Broadway.

One Another for *Each Other*. See *Each Other*.

Only. "He only had one." Say, He had only one, or, better, one only. The other sentence might be taken to mean that only he had one; that, indeed, is what it distinctly says. The correct placing of only in a sentence requires attention and skill.

Opine for *Think*. The word is not very respectably connected.

Opposite for *Contrary*. "I hold the opposite opinion." "The opposite practice."

Or for *Nor*. Probably our most nearly universal solecism. "I cannot see the sun or the moon." This means that I am unable to see one of them, though I may see the other. By using nor, I affirm the invisibility of both, which is what I wanted to do. If a man is not white or black he may nevertheless be a Negro or a Caucasian; but if he is not white nor black he belongs to some other race. See *Neither*.

Ordinarily for *Usually*. Clumsy.

Ovation. In ancient Rome an ovation was an inferior triumph accorded to victors in minor wars or unimportant battle. Its character and limitations, like those of the triumph, were strictly defined by law and custom. An enthusiastic demonstration in honor of an American civilian is nothing like that, and should not be called by its name.

Over for *About, In,* or *Concerning.* "Don't cry over spilt milk." "He rejoiced over his acquittal."

Over for *More than.* "A sum of over ten thousand dollars." "Upward of ten thousand dollars" is equally objectionable.

Over for *On.* "The policeman struck him over the head." If the blow was over the head it did not hit him.

Over with. "Let us have it over with." Omit with. A better expression is, Let us get done with it.

Outside of. Omit the preposition.

Pair for *Pairs.* If a word has a good plural use each form in its place.

Pants for *Trousers.* Abbreviated from pantaloons, which are no longer worn. Vulgar exceedingly.

Partially for *Partly.* A dictionary word, to swell the book.

Party for *Person.* "A party named Brown." The word, used in that sense, has the excuse that it is a word. Otherwise it is no better than "pants" and "gent." A person making an agreement, however, is a party to that agreement.

Patron for *Customer.*

Pay for *Give, Make,* etc. "He pays attention." "She paid a visit to Niagara." It is conceivable that one may owe attention or a visit to another person, but one cannot be indebted to a place.

Pay. "Laziness does not pay." "It does not pay to be un-

civil." This use of the word is grossly commercial. Say,
Indolence is unprofitable. There is no advantage in incivil-
ity.

Peek for *Peep.* Seldom heard in England, though
common here. "I peeked out through the curtain and saw
him." That it is a variant of peep is seen in the child's word
peek-a-boo, equivalent to bo-peep. Better use the senior
word.

Peculiar for *Odd,* or *Unusual.* Also sometimes used to
denote distinction, or particularity. Properly a thing is peculiar only to another thing, of which it is characteristic,
nothing else having it; as knowledge of the use of fire is
peculiar to Man.

People for *Persons.* "Three people were killed." "Many
people are superstitious." People has retained its parity of
meaning with the Latin *populus,* whence it comes, and the
word is not properly used except to designate a population,
or large fractions of it considered in the mass. To speak of
any stated or small number of persons as people is incorrect.

Per. "Five dollars *per* day." "Three *per* hundred." Say,
three dollars a day; three in a hundred. If you must use the
Latin preposition use the Latin noun too: *per diem; per
centum.*

Perpetually for *Continually.* "The child is perpetually
asking questions." What is done perpetually is done continually and forever.

Phenomenal for *Extraordinary,* or *Surprising.* Everything
that occurs is phenomenal, for all that we know about is
phenomena, appearances. Of realities, noumena, we are ignorant.

Plead (pronounced "pled") for *Pleaded.* "He plead
guilty."

Plenty for *Plentiful.* "Fish and fowl were plenty."

Poetess. A foolish word, like "authoress."

Poetry for *Verse.* Not all verse is poetry; not all poetry is verse. Few persons can know, or hope to know, the one from the other, but he who has the humility to doubt (if such a one there be) should say verse if the composition is metrical.

Point Blank. "He fired at him point blank." This usually is intended to mean directly, or at short range. But point blank means the point at which the line of sight is crossed downward by the trajectory—the curve described by the missile.

Poisonous for *Venomous.* Hemlock is poisonous, but a rattlesnake is venomous.

Politics. The word is not plural because it happens to end with s.

Possess for *Have.* "To possess knowledge is to possess power." Possess is lacking in naturalness and unduly emphasizes the concept of ownership.

Practically for *Virtually.* This error is very common. "It is practically conceded." "The decision was practically unanimous." "The panther and the cougar are practically the same animal." These and similar misapplications of the word are virtually without excuse.

Predicate for *Found,* or *Base.* "I predicate my argument on universal experience." What is predicated of something is affirmed as an attribute of it, as omnipotence is predicated of the Deity.

Prejudice for *Prepossession.* Literally, a prejudice is merely a prejudgment—a decision before evidence—and may be favorable or unfavorable, but it is so much more frequently used in the latter sense than in the former that clarity is better got by the other word for reasonless approval.

Preparedness for *Readiness*. An awkward and needless word much used in discussion of national armaments, as, "Our preparedness for war."

Preside. "Professor Swackenhauer presided at the piano." "The deviled crab table was presided over by Mrs. Dooley." How would this sound? "The ginger pop stand was under the administration of President Woolwit, and Professor Sooffle presided at the flute."

Pretend for *Profess*. "I do not pretend to be infallible." Of course not; one does not care to confess oneself a pretender. To pretend is to try to deceive; one may profess quite honestly.

Preventative for *Preventive*. No such word as preventative.

Previous for *Previously*. "The man died previous to receipt of the letter."

Prior to for *Before*. Stilted.

Propose for *Purpose*, or *Intend*. "I propose to go to Europe." A mere intention is not a proposal.

Proposition for *Proposal*. "He made a proposition." In current slang almost anything is a proposition. A difficult enterprise is "a tough proposition," an agile wrestler, "a slippery proposition," and so forth.

Proportions for *Dimensions*. "A rock of vast proportions." Proportions relate to form; dimensions to magnitude.

Proven for *Proved*. Good Scotch, but bad English.

Proverbial for *Familiar*. "The proverbial dog in the manger." The animal is not "proverbial" for it is not mentioned in a proverb, but in a fable.

Quit for *Cease, Stop*. "Jones promises to quit drinking." In another sense, too, the word is commonly misused, as, "He has quit the town." Say, quitted.

Quite. "She is quite charming." If it is meant that she is entirely charming this is right, but usually the meaning intended to be conveyed is less than that—that she is rather, or somewhat, charming.

Raise for *Bring up, Grow, Breed,* etc. In this country a word-of-all-work: "raise children," "raise wheat," "raise cattle." Children are brought up, grain, hay and vegetables are grown, animals and poultry are bred.

Real for *Really,* or *Very.* "It is real good of him." "The weather was real cold."

Realize for *Conceive,* or *Comprehend.* "I could not realize the situation." Writers caring for precision use this word in the sense of to make real, not to make seem real. A dream seems real, but is actually realized when made to come true.

Recollect for *Remember.* To remember is to have in memory; to recollect is to recall what has escaped from memory. We remember automatically; in recollecting we make a conscious effort.

Redeem for *Retrieve.* "He redeemed his good name." Redemption (Latin *redemptio,* from *re* and *dimere*) is allied to ransom, and carries the sense of buying back; whereas to retrieve is merely to recover what was lost.

Redound for *Conduce.* "A man's honesty redounds to his advantage." We make a better use of the word if we say of one (for example) who has squandered a fortune, that its loss redounds to his advantage, for the word denotes a fluctuation, as from seeming evil to actual good; as villification may direct attention to one's excellent character.

Refused. "He was refused a crown." It is the crown that was refused to him. See *Given.*

Regular for *Natural,* or *Customary.* "Flattery of the people is the demagogue's regular means to political preferment." Regular properly relates to a rule (*regula*) more definite than the law of antecedent and consequent.

Reliable for *Trusty*, or *Trustworthy*. A word not yet admitted to the vocabulary of the fastidious, but with a strong backing for the place.

Remit for *Send*. "On receiving your bill I will remit the money." Remit does not mean that; it means give back, yield up, relinquish, etc. It means, also, to cancel, as in the phrase, the remission of sins.

Rendition for *Interpretation*, or *Performance*. "The actor's rendition of the part was good." Rendition means a surrender, or a giving back.

Reportorial. A vile word, improperly made. It assumes the Latinized spelling, "reportor." The Romans had not the word, for they were, fortunately for them, without the thing.

Repudiate for *Deny*. "He repudiated the accusation."

Reside for *Live*. "They reside in Hohokus." Stilted.

Residence for *Dwelling*, or *House*. See *Mansion*.

Respect for *Way*, or *Matter*. "They were alike in that respect." The misuse comes of abbreviating: the sentence properly written might be, They were alike in respect of that—*i.e.*, with regard to that. The word in the bad sense has even been pluralized: "In many respects it is admirable."

Respective. "They went to their respective homes." The adjective here (if an adjective is thought necessary) should be several. In the adverbial form the word is properly used in the sentence following: John and James are bright and dull, respectively. That is, John is bright and James dull.

Responsible. "The bad weather is responsible for much sickness." "His intemperance was responsible for his crime." Responsibility is not an attribute of anything but human beings, and few of these can respond, in damages or otherwise. Responsible is nearly synonymous with accountable and answerable, which, also, are frequently misused.

Restive for *Restless*. These words have directly contrary meanings; the dictionaries' disallowance of their identity would be something to be thankful for, but that is a dream.

Retire for *Go to Bed*. English of the "genteel" sort. See *Genteel*.

Rev. for *The Rev*. "Rev. Dr. Smith."

Reverence for *Revere*.

Ride for *Drive*. On horseback one does drive, and in a vehicle one does ride, but a distinction is needed here, as in England; so, here as there, we may profitably make it, riding in the saddle and driving in the carriage.

Roomer for *Lodger*. See *Bedder* and *Mealer*—if you can find them.

Round for *About*. "They stood round." See *Around*.

Ruination for *Ruin*. Questionably derived and problematically needful.

Run for *Manage*, or *Conduct*. Vulgar—hardly better than slang.

Say for *Voice*. "He had no say in determining the matter." Vulgar.

Scholar for *Student*, or *Pupil*. A scholar is a person who is learned, not a person who is learning.

Score for *Win*, *Obtain*, etc. "He scored an advantage over his opponent." To score is not to win a point, but to record it.

Second-handed for *Second-hand*. There is no such word.

Secure for *Procure*. "He secured a position as book-keeper." "The dwarf secured a stick and guarded the jewels that he had found." Then it was the jewels that were secured.

Seldom ever. A most absurd locution.

Self-confessed. "A self-confessed assassin." Self is superfluous: one's sins cannot be confessed by another.

Sensation for *Emotion.* "The play caused a great sensation." "A sensational newspaper." A sensation is a physical feeling; an emotion, a mental. Doubtless the one usually accompanies the other, but the good writer will name the one that he has in mind, not the other. There are few errors more common than the one here noted.

Sense for *Smell.* "She sensed the fragrance of roses." Society English.

Set for *Sit.* "A setting hen."

Settee for *Settle.* This word belongs to the peasantry of speech.

Settle for *Pay.* "Settle the bill." "I shall take it now and settle for it later."

Shades for *Shade.* "Shades of Noah! how it rained!" "O shades of Caesar!" A shade is a departed soul, as conceived by the ancients; one to each mortal part is the proper allowance.

Show for *Chance,* or *Opportunity.* "He didn't stand a show." Say, He had no chance.

Sick for *Ill.* Good usage now limits this word to cases of nausea, but it is still legitimate in sickly, sickness, love-sick, and the like.

Side for *Agree,* or *Stand.* "I side with the Democrats." "He always sided with what he thought right."

Sideburns for *Burnsides.* A form of whiskers named from a noted general of the civil war, Ambrose E. Burnside. It seems to be thought that the word side has something to do with it, and that as an adjective it should come first, according to our idiom.

Side-hill for *Hillside.* A reasonless transposition for which it is impossible to assign a cause, unless it is abbreviated from side o' the hill.

Sideways for *Sidewise.* See *Endways.*

Since for *Ago.* "He came here not long since and died."

Smart for *Bright,* or *Able.* An Americanism that is dying out. But "smart" has recently come into use for fashionable, which is almost as bad.

Snap for *Period* (of time) or *Spell.* "A cold snap." This is a word of incomprehensible origin in that sense; we can know only that its parents were not respectable. "Spell" is itself not very well-born.

So—as. See *As—as.*

So for *True.* "If you see it in the Daily Livercomplaint it is so." "Is that so?" Colloquial and worse.

Solemnize. This word rightly means to make solemn, not to perform, or celebrate, ceremoniously something already solemn, as a marriage, or a mass. We have no exact synonym, but this explains, rather than justifies, its use.

Some for *Somewhat.* "He was hurt some."

Soon for *Willingly.* "I would as soon go as stay." "That soldier would sooner eat than fight." Say, rather eat.

Space for *Period.* "A long space of time." Space is so different a thing from time that the two do not go well together.

Spend for *Pass.* "We shall spend the summer in Europe." Spend denotes a voluntary relinquishment, but time goes from us against our will.

Square for *Block.* "He lives three squares away." A city block is seldom square.

Squirt for *Spurt.* Absurd.

Stand and *Stand for* for *Endure.* "The patient stands pain well." "He would not stand for misrepresentation."

Standpoint for *Point of View,* or *Viewpoint.*

State for *Say.* "He stated that he came from Chicago." "It is stated that the president is angry." We state a proposition, or a principle, but say that we are well. And we say our prayers—some of us.

Still Continue. "The rain still continues." Omit still; it is contained in the other word.

Stock. "I take no stock in it." Disagreeably commercial. Say, I have no faith in it. Many such metaphorical expressions were unobjectionable, even pleasing, in the mouth of him who first used them, but by constant repetition by others have become mere slang, with all the offensiveness of plagiarism. The prime objectionableness of slang is its hideous lack of originality. Until mouth-worn it is not slang.

Stop for *Stay.* "Prayer will not stop the ravages of cholera." Stop is frequently misused for stay in another sense of the latter word: "He is stopping at the hotel." Stopping is not a continuing act; one cannot be stopping who has already stopped.

Stunt. A word recently introduced and now overworked, meaning a task, or performance in one's trade, or calling,— doubtless a variant of stint, without that word's suggestion of allotment and limitation. It is still in the reptilian stage of evolution.

Subsequent for *Later*, or *Succeeding.* Legitimate enough, but ugly and needless. "He was subsequently hanged." Say, afterward.

Substantiate for *Prove.* Why?

Success. "The project was a success." Say, was successful. Success should not have the indefinite article.

Such Another for *Another Such.* There is illustrious authority for this—in poetry. Poets are a lawless folk, and may do as they please so long as they do please.

Such for *So.* "He had such weak legs that he could not stand." The absurdity of this is made obvious by changing the form of the statement: "His legs were such weak that he could not stand." If the word is an adverb in the one sentence it is in the other. "He is such a great bore that none can endure him." Say, so great a bore.

Suicide. This is never a verb. "He suicided." Say, He killed himself, or He took his own life. See *Commit Suicide.*

Supererogation. To supererogate is to overpay, or to do more than duty requires. But the excess must be in the line of duty; merely needless and irrelevant action is not supererogation. The word is not a natural one, at best.

Sure for *Surely.* "They will come, sure." Slang.

Survive for *Live,* or *Persist.* Survival is an outliving, or outlasting of something else. "The custom survives" is wrong, but a custom may survive its utility. Survive is a transitive verb.

Sustain for *Incur.* "He sustained an injury." "He sustained a broken neck." That means that although his neck was broken he did not yield to the mischance.

Talented for *Gifted.* These are both past participles, but there was once the verb to gift, whereas there was never the verb "to talent." If Nature did not talent a person the person is not talented.

Tantamount for *Equivalent.* "Apology is tantamount to confession." Let this ugly word alone; it is not only illegitimate, but ludicrously suggests catamount.

Tasty for *Tasteful.* Vulgar.

Tear Down for *Pull Down.* "The house was torn down." This is an indigenous solecism; they do not say so in England.

Than Whom. See *Whom.*

The. A little word that is terribly overworked. It is needlessly affixed to names of most diseases: "the cholera," "the smallpox," "the scarlet fever," and such. Some escape it: we do not say, "the sciatica," nor "the locomotor ataxia." It is too common in general propositions, as, "The payment of interest is the payment of debt." "The virtues that are automatic are the best." "The tendency to falsehood should be checked." "Kings are not under the control of the law." It is impossible to note here all forms of this misuse, but a page of almost any book will supply abundant instance. We do not suffer so abject slavery to the definite article as the French, but neither do we manifest their spirit of rebellion by sometimes cutting off the oppressor's tail. One envies the Romans, who had no article, definite or indefinite.

The Following. "Washington wrote the following." The following what? Put in the noun. "The following animals are ruminants." It is not the animals that follow, but their names.

The Same. "They cooked the flesh of the lion and ate the same." "An old man lived in a cave, and the same was a cripple." In humorous composition this may do, though it is not funny; but in serious work use the regular pronoun.

Then as an Adjective. "The then governor of the colony." Say, the governor of the colony at that time.

Those Kind for *That Kind.* "Those kind of things." Almost too absurd for condemnation, and happily not very common out of the class of analphabets.

Though for *If.* "She wept as though her heart was broken." Many good writers, even some devoid of the lexicographers' passion for inclusion and approval, have specifically defended this locution, backing their example by their precept. Perhaps it is a question of taste; let us attend their cry and pass on.

Thrifty for *Thriving.* "A thrifty village." To thrive is an end; thrift is a means to that end.

Through for *Done.* "The lecturer is through talking." "I am through with it." Say, I have done with it.

To. As part of an infinitive it should not be separated from the other part by an adverb, as, "to hastily think," for hastily to think, or, to think hastily. Condemnation of the split infinitive is now pretty general, but it is only recently that any one seems to have thought of it. Our forefathers and we elder writers of this generation used it freely and without shame—perhaps because it had not a name, and our crime could not be pointed out without too much explanation.

To for *At.* "We have been to church." "I was to the theater." One can go to a place, but one cannot be to it.

Total. "The figures totaled 10,000." Say, The total of the figures was 10,000.

Transaction for *Action,* or *Incident.* "The policeman struck the man with his club, but the transaction was not reported." "The picking of a pocket is a criminal transaction." In a transaction two or more persons must have an active or assenting part; as, a business transaction, Transactions of the Geographical Society, etc. The Society's action would be better called Proceedings.

Transpire for *Occur, Happen,* etc. "This event transpired in 1906." Transpire (*trans,* through, and *spirare,* to breathe) means leak out, that is, become known. What transpired in 1906 may have occurred long before.

Trifling for *Trivial.* "A trifling defect"; "a trifling error."

Trust for *Wealthy Corporation.* There are few trusts; capitalists have mostly abandoned the trust form of combination.

Try an Experiment. An experiment is a trial; we cannot try a trial. Say, make.

Try and for *Try to.* "I will try and see him." This plainly says that my effort to see him will succeed—which I cannot know and do not wish to affirm. "Please try and come." This colloquial slovenliness of speech is almost universal in this country, but freedom of speech is one of our most precious possessions.

Ugly for *Ill-natured, Quarrelsome.* What is ugly is the temper, or disposition, not the person having it.

Under-handed and *Under-handedly* for *Under-hand*. See *Off-handed*.

Unique. "This is very unique." "The most unique house in the city." There are no degrees of uniqueness: a thing is unique if there is not another like it. The word has nothing to do with oddity, strangeness, nor picturesqueness.

United States as a Singular Noun. "The United States is for peace." The fact that we are in some ways one nation has nothing to do with it; it is enough to know that the word States is plural—if not, what is State? It would be pretty hard on a foreigner skilled in the English tongue if he could not venture to use our national name without having made a study of the history of our Constitution and political institutions. Grammar has not a speaking acquaintance with politics, and patriotic pride is not schoolmaster to syntax.

Unkempt for *Disordered, Untidy,* etc. Unkempt means uncombed, and can properly be said of nothing but the hair.

Use for *Treat.* "The inmates were badly used." "They use him harshly."

Utter for *Absolute, Entire,* etc. Utter has a damnatory signification and is to be used of evil things only. It is correct to say utter misery, but not "utter happiness;" utterly bad, but not "utterly good."

Various for *Several.* "Various kinds of men." Kinds are various of course, for they vary—that is what makes them kinds. Use various only when, in speaking of a number of things, you wish to direct attention to their variety—their difference, one from another. "The dividend was distributed among the various stockholders." The stockholders vary, as do all persons, but that is irrelevant and was not in mind. "Various persons have spoken to me of you." Their variation is unimportant; what is meant is that there was a small indefinite number of them; that is, several.

Ventilate for *Express, Disclose,* etc. "The statesman ventilated his views." A disagreeable and dog-eared figure of speech.

Verbal for *Oral.* All language is verbal, whether spoken or written, but audible speech is oral. "He did not write, but communicated his wishes verbally." It would have been a verbal communication, also, if written.

Vest for *Waistcoat.* This is American, but as all Americans are not in agreement about it it is better to use the English word.

Vicinity for *Vicinage,* or *Neighborhood.* "He lives in this vicinity." If neither of the other words is desired say, He lives in the vicinity of this place, or, better, He lives near by.

View of. "He invested with the view of immediate profit." "He enlisted with the view of promotion." Say, with a view to.

Vulgar for *Immodest, Indecent.* It is from *vulgus,* the common people, the mob, and means both common and unrefined, but has no relation to indecency.

Way for *Away.* "Way out at sea." "Way down South."

Ways for *Way.* "A squirrel ran a little ways along the road." "The ship looked a long ways off." This surprising word calls loudly for depluralization.

Wed for *Wedded.* "They were wed at noon." "He wed her in Boston." The word wed in all its forms as a substitute for marry, is pretty hard to bear.

Well. As a mere meaningless prelude to a sentence this word is overtasked. "Well, I don't know about that." "Well, you may try." "Well, have your own way."

Wet for *Wetted.* See *Bet.*

Where for *When*. "Where there is reason to expect criticism write discreetly."

Which for *That*. "The boat which I engaged had a hole in it." But a parenthetical clause may rightly be introduced by which; as, The boat, which had a hole in it, I nevertheless engaged. Which and that are seldom interchangeable; when they are, use that. It sounds better.

Whip for *Chastise*, or *Defeat*. To whip is to beat with a whip. It means nothing else.

Whiskers for *Beard*. The whisker is that part of the beard that grows on the cheek. See *Chin Whiskers*.

Who for *Whom*. "Who do you take me for?"

Whom for *Who*. "The man whom they thought was dead is living." Here the needless introduction of was entails the alteration of whom to who. "Remember whom it is that you speak of." "George Washington, than whom there was no greater man, loved a jest." The misuse of whom after than is almost universal. Who and whom trip up many a good writer, although, unlike which and who, they require nothing but knowledge of grammar.

Widow Woman. Omit woman.

Will and *shall*. Proficiency in the use of these apparently troublesome words must be sought in text-books on grammar and rhetoric, where the subject will be found treated with a more particular attention, and at greater length, than is possible in a book of the character of this. Briefly and generally, in the first person, a mere intention is indicated by shall, as, I shall go; whereas will denotes some degree of compliance or determination, as, I will go—as if my going had been requested or forbidden. In the second and the third person, will merely forecasts, as, You (or he) will go; but shall implies something of promise, permission or compulsion by the speaker, as, You (or he) shall go. Another and less obvious compulsion—that of circumstance—

speaks in shall, as sometimes used with good effect: In Germany you shall not turn over a chip without uncovering a philosopher. The sentence is barely more than indicative, shall being almost, but not quite, equivalent to can.

Win out. Like its antithesis, "lose out," this reasonless phrase is of sport, "sporty."

Win for *Won.* "I went to the race and win ten dollars." This atrocious solecism seems to be unknown outside the world of sport, where may it ever remain.

Without for *Unless.* "I cannot go without I recover." Peasantese.

Witness for *See.* To witness is more than merely to see, or observe; it is to observe, and to tell afterward.

Would-be. "The would-be assassin was arrested." The word doubtless supplies a want, but we can better endure the want than the word. In the instance of the assassin, it is needless, for he who attempts to murder is an assassin, whether he succeeds or not.

Index